GW01460210

The Visible a
Worlds of GOD

The Visible and Invisible Worlds of GOD

Caroline Cory

iUniverse, Inc.

New York Lincoln Shanghai

The Visible and Invisible Worlds of GOD

iUniverse books may be ordered through booksellers or by contacting:

iUniverse
2021 Pine Lake Road, Suite 100
Lincoln, NE 68512
www.iuniverse.com
1-800-Authors (1-800-288-4677)

For more information about this book, please visit:
www.omniumfoundation.com

ISBN: 0-595-33343-5

Printed in the United States of America

<u>This book is dedicated to…</u>

My Divine Father

Contents

<u>ACKNOWLEDGMENTS...</u>

To The Assembly of 7 & 12, Antoine, Edwar, Virgyle, Mu, Ashira, Celestine, Astarte, my brother Gabriel,

Beloved John and Linda, thank you for your love and support.

INTRODUCTION

This book is a compilation of thoughts originating from my psyche as well as others'.

Let me explain…

At the age of five, I encountered my first invisible friend. He didn't have a name but I clearly remember the day he stood by me and observed the pitiful spectacle of a Christmas Eve tradition in our living room. While I wondered what the fuss was about and how the Christmas tree related to the birth of Jesus, my friend and I noticed the irony in everyone's behavior: my parents fought while others were busy doing frivolous things. I sadly thought that they were missing the point and that human spirituality seemed lost in a set of meaningless traditions and rituals.

My invisible and compassionate friend stood there and told me to "ask" for things. For example, if I wanted to remember clearly this very moment, I should just "ask". And so I did. Now, thirty five years later, this image is crystal clear in my mind as if it were yesterday—and so is the idea, to just ask.

My friend went on to teach me telepathic communication so we could communicate in the future. He explained that putting the words together and saying them fast enough would form one concept rather than individual letters or words. This was my first attempt at telepathy. At the age of five, it made perfect sense!

As we walked down the street for the midnight Mass, I remember thinking that this was a really important event for me. I could possibly encounter more invisible friends who were truly loving and wise. However, as we entered the elegant establishment, I could only notice my mental solitude within the loud crowd. On this special night, I desperately looked for truthful love and divine wisdom but instead, everyone merrily repeated what seemed to be insignificant incantations. At age five, that did not make sense.

That peculiar evening ended when my invisible friend parted reminding me of the time "we would be together again". He was so loving and wise…Why did he have to leave?

I must have been 6 or 7 years old when my second "evolved" experience occurred. The maid had laid a sharp mirror on a table in my brother's bedroom while she was doing house work. I stood by the door and thought to myself that it was quite irresponsible for "these adults" to leave dangerous sharp objects unprotected when a child— me—was running around the house! I wondered if I "accidentally" cut myself with that mirror whether such an act would be premonitions or "conscious creating". To prove my point, I instinctively walked into the room, bumped into the table and cut my leg open right above my left knee. At that point, the conscious 6-year old child took over as I heard myself shriek uncontrollably. Later on, after a visit to the emergency room, the question about "conscious creating" popped into my head again, at which time my invisible teacher-friend appeared and said: "This is no premonition. You created it. You create everything with your "*thoughts*". At age six, I seemed to know about conscious creating!

About my "thoughts"…

As I grew up, it became clear to me that my thoughts were not all the same: some belonged to my conscious mind while others originated from a more evolved awareness. It was easy to make that distinction due to the type of information I was receiving. The thoughts belonging to my daily conscious mind dealt with mundane things like school, friends, clothes and food, while those originating from the more evolved state dealt with Universal Laws, the mystery of Creation and the existence of God. The conscious part of my psyche was indeed attached to another more mature part, a Super-Conscious or "Higher Self" as some prefer to call it.

With time, I understood that my Higher Self or Spirit Self, as I prefer to call it, was the portion of my psyche communicating with my invisible childhood teachers and friends. More importantly, I realized that it did not exist "independently". Rather, it was merged with another much greater and highly evolved *Massive Consciousness*. There are no words to describe my "blended" feeling with this vast Consciousness other than through personal experience. I can only say that it is very real and very familiar. You encounter no boundaries or limitations there, no duality, polarity or fear. It is a state of perpetual and pure positive energy. It is indeed what we call Divine Bliss and Love.

From that point on, I began the conscious exercise of retrieving messages from my Spirit Self portion and from those other beings who appeared every now and then with different pertinent lessons and information. This group of beings eventually identified themselves as "Source Energy". They form an Assembly which originates at the "Creator-Source" or the "God-Source", and can connect with our human psyche through a consciousness we call "The Cosmic Mind". Each being within this Assembly comprises 70 million entities even though I could only experience and perceive them as 7 or at times 12.

My communions with this massive consciousness were utterly exquisite, yet quite trying. It is through them that I now walk the physical realm hearing and speaking with my Spirit Self and spirit beings as I do with other humans. I eventually realized that this full awareness and interaction with the divine IS the process of self-realization: the ultimate blending with Source Energy. I have therefore dedicated another publication entirely to record these experiences and teachings (to be published in 2005). The book you are reading however, serves the purpose of reorganizing thoughts and vibrations so you may begin to *perceive* the universal organization and *plan* your ascending journey accordingly.

Eventually, my invisible guides unfalteringly referred to me as "their vibrational match in this physical system" and "their spirit family member". What? What could that mean?! I struggled with those thoughts until I began focusing on the material rather than my role or status in the communication process.

I continued questioning and doubting the course of naturally retrieving information from this impressive but invisible source until I began experiencing spontaneous healings. The first healing I recall occurred about 15 years ago. As I laid in bed shivering uncontrollably with a high fever, I decided to ask my aches and pains to stop. Suddenly, the throbbing in my head, the soreness in my throat, the pain in my muscles and joints, the overall helpless and miserable feelings simply vanished, along with the high fever. All this occurred abruptly and without warning. I was amazed and shocked, but managed to quickly dismiss this incident as a lucky coincidence.

These spontaneous healings continued manifesting enough times as to convince me that I was not imagining things and that these events were no coincidence. To make their point, my spirit teachers provoked some healings that were visual and quite dramatic at times, such as the shrinking of a lump on my wrist or the rapid fading of large blisters right before my eyes. Eventually, I came to terms with these extraordinary events and began to wonder if I was able to heal others as I healed myself. Guided by my Psychology background but more importantly this Source Energy I embodied, I was in time able to help many individuals overcome acute and chronic challenges, both physical and emotional. However, the dilemma remained: how to make this priceless reality "credible" and accepted by a society that relies on facts and proofs.

My spirit friends ignored my mortal quandary and went on divulging their truths. They explained that evolutionary physical beings were created by a Creator Consciousness. The human species as well as other material beings that inhabit the planets of this galaxy and beyond are created by the Creator Consciousness, which is the combination of a Divine Creator (a Creator "Father") and a Creator Energy (a Creator "Mother"). Together, they form a massive Body of Light and Consciousness which encompass all evolutionary life.

I further came to understand that our Creation occurs through the deliberate action and focused thought of this Creator Consciousness (our Divine Creator in conjunction with the Creator Energy). Particles "spilt off" from their massive body of Light and materialize as divine and celestial beings, solar and planetary systems and intelligent evolutionary beings, in that order. Therefore all created material beings and things, including humans, carry an infinitesimal part of their original Creator in different composition and proportions. At no time, can we be separate from our Divine Creator. While we are visiting planet Earth with our physical bodies, we remain perpetually attached to Him through an energetic "umbilical cord", as well as through our Spirit Self. It is therefore primordial to our understanding that we perceive reality and all our experiences in terms of ENERGY.

This book finally came together as a result of hundreds of such message downloads. While I realize that my conscious mind is the one translating these concepts into legible English sentences, I opted to keep the text in its third person form as it originated from the higher portions of my psyche as well as from this incredibly vast consciousness, the Source Energy and the Cosmic Mind. The format is also meant to convey a more expanded perspective of reality in order to empower you, the reader, and inspire you to seek deeply for your own Truth.

I should also explain that this book is the reflection of ONE THOUGHT or one idea. One thought from such a source or perspective equals a hundred or so pages in the English language. It is therefore recommended to read the entire book throughout as the questions which will arise in one chapter will most likely be answered in another, or at least at the very end. The text is purposely concise, specific and unstructured all at once. It can be read front to back, back to front or in non-sequenced segments as all contained information form ONE over-all concept from which you will draw you own assessments. Part II, however, offers practical tools that you may apply and utilize in your daily life according to the principles conferred. It is highly advisable to grasp and digest the concepts discussed in the first part of the book in order to benefit more fully from the proposed practical exercises.

Finally, this book is a direct and spontaneous revelation from spirit beings to one in physical form. It is a proof in itself that any willing man or woman is capable of accessing divine knowledge and healing directly and spontaneously. It also provides a unique roadmap of the invisible worlds you live in, beginning with your life in human form—with the ultimate destination of the Creator-Source from which you have sprung.

Enjoy this journey and make no judgment. If this text managed to make it into your hands, it is purposely so. It may become sacred or simply remain a practical tool for your own self-realization. In any case, Love and Blessings are encoded herein.

PART I

Philosophy or Truth

1

All Existence Is Energy

The following material appeared in segments over a period of 2 to 3 months. My spirit guardians were adamant about me grasping the concept that all that I see, feel, eat or dream is a form of energy because "that is the core of all knowledge" they insisted. During this time period, they continuously appeared to remind me that what I had just experienced was energetic manifestation. With their help, I began to see lines and grids that related our planet to other systems and galaxies. They drew my attention to specific locations on the globe that represented different physical and mathematical links to the nucleus of our Universe and beyond. While I had no scientific background and did not quite understand the process, I was nonetheless able to comprehend such a concept through these perceptual experiences and through inner "know-sis", as they called it. Humans have such an ability and regardless of our scientific proficiency, the truths presented herein are irrefutable. In response to my doubts and questioning, my invisible teachers tirelessly reflected Einstein's image in my consciousness, mentioning repeatedly that "he also just knew...His work was simply to prove it."

◆   ◆   ◆

The physical worlds, planetary systems and universes are connected through energetic and electromagnetic lines and grids which overlap in such a way as to unite homogeneously. They all converge at one Source, the original Universal Creator-Source from which all Life springs. No world can be sustained outside these energetic fields or without the rhythmic breath and pulse of this Creator-Source.

The energetic grids have several functions which include establishing and maintaining gravitational forces, interplanetary communication and broadcasts, vehicle transportation and time separation.

GRAVITATIONAL GRIDS...

All planets, solar systems, galaxies and universes are created simultaneously. While scientists may still consider their physical movement and evolution to be chaotic, they are all, in fact, in perfect cosmic order and arrangement. Their systematic gravitational forces maintain a perfect harmonic balance in relation with one another and with their original Creator-Source. The organized gravitational forces of all physical systems and intelligent life are indeed eternal, indestructible and infinitely connected to each other and to the one Creator-Source.

Your planet's gravitational and electromagnetic grid is located approximately 7,000 miles from Earth and forms a perfect spherical matrix around its surface. These electromagnetic systems continue on to outer layers of physical space, to balance each neighboring planet and star system. The Earth's grids and energetic lines form a matrix which contains ALL human, physical, "mind-al" and spiritual patterns. Through these grids, you are energetically connected with all other beings and things including the Earth itself from which you have sprung.

All existence, physical and non-physical, has consciousness to a varying degree and due to its electromagnetic nature, it must travel and communicate through energetic lines. A Thought or a Force, for example, has a vibrational frequency which requires the use of grids and matrixes to travel from one physical point to another. Thought is communicated within your planet, and with other planets, galaxies and universes through these energetic lines. While invisible to you, these communications and broadcasts are actual and incessant allowing the maintenance of a Thought/Mind balance within your planet and your neighboring worlds.

COMMUNICATION AND TRANSPORTATION GRIDS...

The energetic grids on your planet are arranged in such a way as to allow communication with other worlds, physical and non-physical. The transfer of Thought occurs through these grids: Divine Beings monitor such communication to ensure spiritual expansion of the species, while you knowingly or unknowingly transfer thoughts with other human and non-human entities and call it synchronicity or telepathy.

Similar to Thought travel, Celestial Beings and Forces require transport vehicles and routes to commute between the worlds. Interplanetary, intergalactic and universal transports are made possible through grids aligned in such a way as to connect the different physical areas you can be transported to. While similar concepts already exist in your science-fiction world, they are nonetheless real and necessary for the evolution and expansion of all intelligent beings within the Cosmos.

Throughout your history, Earth has experienced the visitation of extra-terrestrial and Super-human intelligent beings. These visitations are also made possible through the grid lines established to transport and convert consciousness of elevated frequencies. When certain planetary and star alignments occur, the grid lines of the respective worlds are in a precise configuration as to permit a specific energetic exchange. The arrival or landing of Super-human Beings on your planet occurs at such propitious times.

While grid lines converge at different points of the Earth matrix, only one site on your planet is considered to be the "umbilical cord" that connects you to the nucleus of your Universe, where your planetary Divine Creators and Divine Guardians reside. That site is located approximately at the 33 to 35-degree latitude and the 33 to 35-degree longitude conjunction points of your planet and is considered the only possible entry and exit point for Super-human and Divine Beings. This area corresponds to your current Middle Eastern countries, namely Israel and Lebanon. However, due to the continuous galactic movements and axis shifts which affect your planet approximately every 20,000 years, this conjunction point was once located over ancient Mesopotamia and is still in motion. Since these divine doorways are the most charged electromagnetically, they will also allow the occurrence and strong acceleration of all human energy, positive or negative. The conflicts you are currently observing in these areas are particularly significant to the overall human economic, sociological, religious and political stability. However, due to their energetic supercharge, violent clashes in these mystical areas will remain hopelessly incessant.

It is important to recognize however that the current axis shift is of an unusual nature and will be setting the Earth in a new configuration which will re-align all entry and access points with your divine creators' headquarters. Your latest planetary alignment in 2003 was the final factor necessary to complete the locking so to speak of your planet's position within the Cosmos. While it will perpetually adjust and shift, Earth's energetic doors have now been opened, which established your new era and, hence, freed your planet from its long isolation.

TIME SEPARATION GRIDS...

Linear time, as observed on Earth, is a necessary physical agreement which divides your space. Time is then a function of the space you occupy and is distributed in different areas of your planet in such a way as to appear progressive. Yet, this phenomenon is a distortion of physical perception. You may utilize energetic alignments and electromagnetic grids to suspend time, which means you can exist without linear time within these alignment points. What you call "time travel" is nothing but the passage through these lines and the experience of time suspension. Your observations of space from your limited Earthly perspective have not caught up, so to speak, with the original "timing" of your universe and planet creation. For example, you have only discovered, a planet within your solar system a few years ago which, is in fact, billions of years old. Your linear time is responsible for this delayed perception in relation to Creation.

By definition, Energy is vibrational. When the vibrational frequency of Energy is low enough as to appear static, it is then called matter. When it vibrates at higher velocities, its composing particles are altered and therefore become invisible. Vortices are energetic juncture-points which allow the acceleration or alteration of the vibrational frequency of the subject being exposed to it. For example, if a material object is placed within a juncture point of electromagnetic vortices, the object's vibrational frequency will accelerate or be altered to such a point as to disappear. Yet, the object, in fact, still exists in another frequency range which cannot be perceived by the restricted vision of the human eye.

Such is also the reason for the mysterious disappearance of airplanes or boats which accidentally cross these vortex points and are unable to rematerialize within the time/space continuum of the rest of the Earth plane. These objects and beings have not disintegrated nor destructed. They simply continue existing in another vibrational frequency undetected by human perception.

While some scholars have succeeded in determining the location of certain vortex areas charged with tremendous electro-magnetism, it is not necessary to gain this knowledge in order to attain an evolved state of consciousness or self-realization. It is important, however, to recognize that these alignment points balance your planet perfectly with the rest of the surrounding universe and that the planet's constant shifting will continue altering the precise position of these energetic lines.

HOW TO DEFINE "ENERGY"...

Energy does not equal force. What you call Force is condensed, focused and specialized energy. Force is created and always manipulated and controlled by Mind Energy.

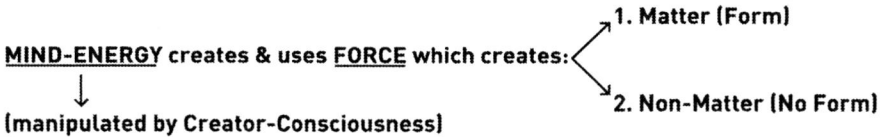

MIND-ENERGY creates & uses **FORCE** which creates:

↓

(manipulated by Creator-Consciousness)

1. **Matter (Form)**

2. **Non-Matter (No Form)**

FIGURE 1: Energy Definition

ENERGY MANIFESTATION...

Energy (which can also be Light, Sound or Heat), can manifest as: 1. Physical Matter 2. Mind-Energy or 3. Spirit-Energy.

These various manifestations of Energy are dependant on the rate of its vibrational frequency (speed), the type of its composing elements (mass) and the shape of the rotation around its core (character).

PHYSICAL MATTER and the physical worlds are created by the Creator-Mind. They are the by-product of focused and specialized Thought of an evolved Consciousness-Mind, capable of manipulating energy in such a way as to make it appear physical and static. This evolved Consciousness-Mind can mold and alter the vibrational frequency of Energy into an idea, a star system, a planet or an evolutionary species. While this Consciousness-Mind becomes the Creator of its physical world, this physical manifestation is an extension of it and not an entity separate or independent from it. All matter is an extension of its manipulator. It is the Mind of its Creator "slowed down", figuratively speaking.

The physical worlds, while appearing static, are vibratory energy: therefore, they have a consciousness. Planets and star systems where intelligent beings dwell are also considered conscious beings, each with a different set of properties and characteristics. They are living creations which interact energetically with you and the rest of the cosmos through their own "intelligence" and consciousness-mind. Your planet is just as alive as you are, as she breaths, pulsates, consumes and detoxifies at the divine rhythms of the Consciousness that created her.

THE MIND-ENERGY creates and controls matter. It is the creative engine behind all creation. The mind can recognize, discern, choose, focus and force Energy into manifestation. The Creator-Mind or Consciousness creates by splitting its energetic particles into material or intelligent manifestation, and thus ALL which it creates becomes an extension of it. Physical and intelligent creations are energetically intertwined within the Creator-Mind, who is also their manipulator and controller.

The created mind requires manipulation and control in order to preserve balance between the created species and the Creator-Source. This is not interference or manipulation of free-will. Rather, it is an energetic cleansing or "virus-scanning" system which maintains cosmic balance. The Mind Controllers are divine beings assigned to all evolutionary physical worlds for the purpose of mind-thought balance and evolution. As you think, you broadcast emotions and intents which correlate with a frequency the Mind Controllers can minister to. If the pulsation and vibration frequency of your collective consciousness reaches a level of imbalance, these beings are able to extrapolate those harmful and negative tendencies and restore the harmonic balance with the rest the Universe. While you may still experience evil and disharmony within your world, the global consciousness is nonetheless controlled and perpetually maintained within the galactic order.

THE SPIRIT-ENERGY is the breath or pulse of the Creator-Source which sustains all life throughout the cosmos. When you breathe, so does all space as you watch the entire cosmos expand and retract; when your heart beats, so do all divine beings as they hold a universal pulse and harmonic rhythm throughout the entire cosmos. You are indeed a particle of the Spirit-Energy of the Creator-Source itself, perpetually breathing and pulsating at the rhythm of the entire Creation.

Created beings, which come into existence through the deliberate thought and action of the evolved consciousness of a Creator-Mind, can manifest as material, transitory or purely spiritual. The rate of their vibrational frequency determines their state of manifestation: if their vibrational level is low, they will appear material. If their vibrational rate is high, they will remain in a spirit state. Therefore, spirit must lower its vibratory frequency to such a point as to become physical. Such is the process by which your spirit incarnates into a material human body.

All aspects of existence, matter, mind or spirit, are intricately associated as one is an extension of the other. No phenomenon in the universe can be explained without the consideration of all 3 aspects of existence simultaneously. When you attempt to identify the characteristics and nature of your physical body, your physical planet or your physical universe without the consideration of their mind and spirit components, you are only observing a portion of their entirety. Under those circumstances, a full grasp of the true nature, the mechanism and the reasons of your physical worlds will never be achieved nor replicated. They are a fact and universal law indeed. We may conclude by asserting that all Existence is Energy-manifestation in different forms. In other words, Energy is all aspects of Existence or Energy IS the "All That Exists": that which you call "God".

2

A Universe in the Making

The following material came as the logical sequence for the information in the previous chapter. If all existence was energy and our planet was linked to the nucleus of a universe, well then, how many universes are there and how do they all connect? What is "the Source" and where is it located anyway? While I asked these questions, I could not help feeling intimidated by such an attempt considering my ignorance and inexperience in astronomy, physics etc...After all, these subjects are for the Brian Greens, the Carl Sagans and the Stephen Hawkins who are experts in their fields and dedicate their lives to uncovering such matters. In the midst of my constant feelings of inadequacy and insecurity, my spirit friends reminded me that the majority of humans currently on Earth also do not comprehend such truths—even those scientists I was in awe of! In that sense, I was the perfect candidate for carrying the message and relaying it onto others.

Just in case, I hastily subscribed to "Scientific American" and diligently began following programs and lectures on cosmology research and astronomical exploration. Of course, that only added to my confusion as I realized that science did not offer any solutions. Rather, it was all merely speculative. If anything, it really seemed to be catching up with what I already knew! Over a period of 6 months of frantic scientific pursuit, my invisible friends waited patiently as I believed I would be revealed some incredible mathematical equations of some sort, "explaining" the Universe.

When I finally came to my senses, they expectantly appeared and said: "You are here to experience life from a human perspective and reveal Divine Truth as it is revealed to you. The knowledge of Creation is based on the knowledge of the Creator, not on the physical aspects of your planetary system or the universe."

◆   ◆   ◆

The physical universes are organized in such a way as to perpetually gravitate around the nucleus of all Creation, the Creator-Source or the physical land mass of Paradise. Each Major Universe consists of millions of Minor Universes. Within each Minor Universe are billions of galaxies, within which are billions of planetary and solar systems. Each Minor Universe also has its own gravitational nucleus established in the perfect image of all other nucleuses and therefore shares similar physical characteristics.

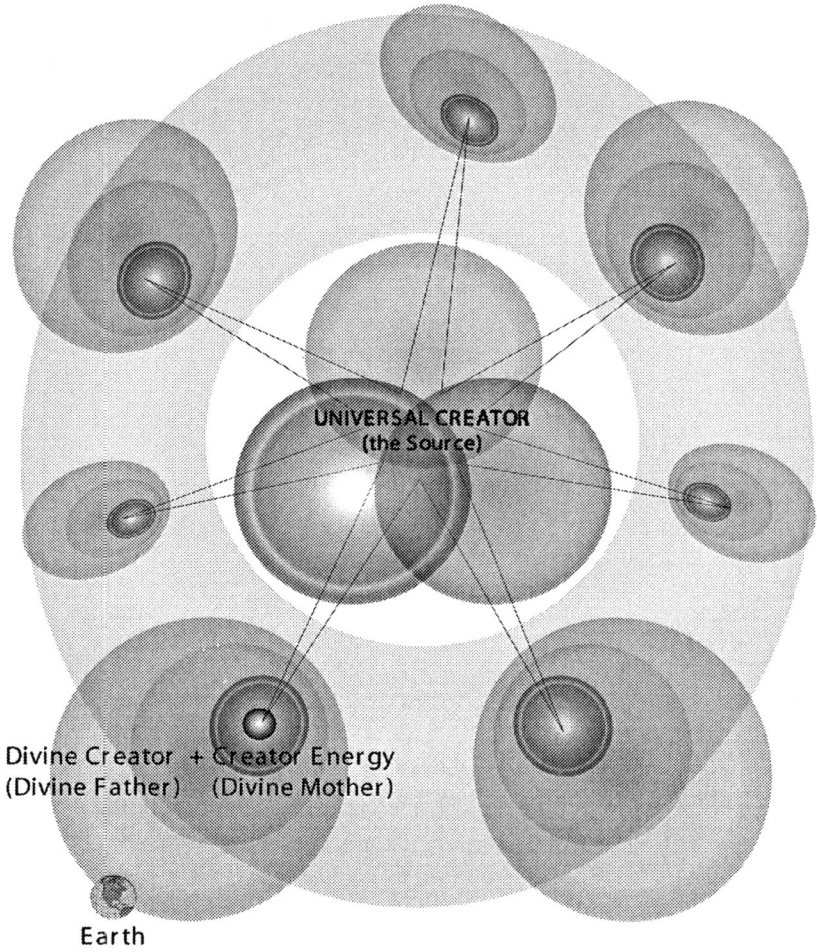

UNIVERSAL CREATOR
(the Source)

Divine Creator + Creator Energy
(Divine Father)   (Divine Mother)

Earth

FIGURE 2: Multi-Universe organization around the Creator-Source

Your planet belongs to the most "recently" created Major Universe, which is still unfinished. It sits at one of the furthest point from Paradise and the Creator-Source. This by no means implies that Earth is any less attended to, as your Divine Creator energy is distributed throughout its far-flung creation <u>equally</u>. This simply means that the species inhabiting these remote planets have more ground to conquer, so to speak, in terms of consciousness expansion in order to attain its purest form of divinity.

The COSMIC MIND (which is the Mind-Energy of the Creator-Source) is funneled and can be experienced through the Mind-Energy of your Divine Creator within your system. Expanding and blending your mind and spirit with your Divine Creator's is the way by which spiritual perfection is attained.

The Cosmic Mind is the gravitational Mind force which pulls all of creation towards the Creator-Source. It is comprised of the 7 aspects of the Creator-Source (Universal Creator/Mind; Universal Body; Universal Spirit and their respective combinations) and represents their nature and function. Each aspect supervises one Major Universe and gives it its respective characteristics.

The Cosmic Mind is the Mind Energy of the Creator-Source which is then expressed and experienced through the Divine Creators of the 7 different Major Universes. Your Major Universe is created by a Divine Creator who is also a Divine "Father" in conjunction with a Creator Energy who is your Divine "Mother". Together they distribute the Mind Energy of the Creator-Source throughout your entire system and thereby define your intellectual and spiritual functioning and nature.

The MIND ENERGY present in your system is distributed evenly throughout your sphere and indwells all evolutionary beings equally. It conjoins the energetic grids around your planets, approximately 7,000 miles about the surface of the Earth. Its gravitational force, which pulls your collective mind matrix towards the nucleus of your universe, is what compels you to "find God". It is what shapes your belief system in what you perceive as Truth and Goodness. It is the innate urge to evolve and blend with the greater consciousness of your Divine Creator. Finally, it is the gravitational energy through which you can ultimately find and blend with the Creator-Source of all existence, and that is "God".

THE CREATOR-SOURCE ETERNALLY SELF-CREATES...

The Major Universes are in constant creation and will continue self-creating eternally. The Creator-Source has no end and it never had a beginning. Nothing exists outside the Creator-Source.

All that exists is in a state of "becoming" except Divine Truths, which are absolute. There are divine laws, mathematical and physical laws to explain the universe. However, all laws equal one formula and all formulas are contained in the one Creator-Source. All laws and all formulas ARE the Creator-Source who is thus the amalgamation of all truths and realities. This is indeed an evolving universe, unfinished and eternally self-creating.

The Creator-Source is not one being or one person. It is a layered, multi-dimensional existence. It is also an idea, a concept that the created being refers to as an explanation of Creation and Life. There are as many interpretations of what "God" is as there are living beings on one planet. While you may congregate in different religions in an attempt to grasp the concept of God and Creation, each one of you has an innate unique genetic arrangement which allows you a distinct experience of reality, including the concept of God or the Creator-Source. And as your consciousness evolves, so does your concept and idea of what God is. But if God is infinite, so will be your quest of who He is.

You are one minute particle of the Creator-Source's far-flung and infinite consciousness. Therefore, you are created and born with the knowledge of who He is just as each minute particle of the whole, while having its own individuality and consciousness, is capable of visualizing and remembering the whole. You are able to remember and recreate the events of your physical birth, which is your "split" from your Divine Creator. Because your essence is made partially of your Creator's energetic material, you are continuously drawn to remembering your true essence and the process by which you came about. Becoming one with the Creator-Source simply means remembering and recognizing the particle in you which is a fraction of the Divine whole. This very remembrance IS your re-unification or blending with your Divine Creator.

The Creator of a universe expresses Himself through His creations. As you evolve, so does His knowledge of you and your experiences.

When you expand your creative and procreative skills, you are enabled to continue on an eternal journey of Life. You can create perpetually and indefinitely in one form of another—and as you do, the universe unravels its myriad dimensions and layers to you and continues to offer new opportunities for creation. The Universe evolves eternally and so you may say that you, as consciousness, are an eternal creation which is never complete, never finished.

SCIENCE EXPLAINING THE INFINITE...

Those scientists who look to define Existence and Life with a set of finite formulas may be missing the point if they realized that finite can only measure finite. The world of infinite encompasses all things, including numbers and formulas. The language of the infinite is <u>vibratory</u> and the Creation formula of the infinite is an ENERGY, not a number.

This Energy is equivalent to vibratory sound and frequency which also equal a mathematical formula and atomic element. The Divine Energy IS atomic and physical manifestation. However, to say that knowing the mathematical formula is to understand the creation process by which this Divine Energy comes about is erroneous indeed. For the understanding of Creation is based on the knowledge of the Creator. No mere scientific formula can lead to the knowledge of an infinite Being or unravel the mystery of Creation. Quite the contrary, it is the knowledge of the Infinite Being that will define His infinite potential as well as the endless possibility of all formulas and potential manifestations.

The Creator-Source of all beings and things is the One Source and Being where all Life merges in one original formula called Divine LOVE. The word "love" is also a vibratory sound and an atomic manifestation. Its associated mathematical numbers equal <u>infinity</u>. Divine Love can never equal a finite and final formula as it is infinite indeed. Yet, it is the creative formula of the Creator-Source and its respective Divine Order.

Even your physical worlds, which appear to be finite, are energetically associated with all which exists. They are therefore a finite extension of an infinite Creator. Their mathematical formulas cannot be realized without the understanding of their infinite Creator. When scientists base their reasoning on the characteristics of the physical universe alone, they can only attain knowledge pertaining to its physicality. The work of Creation is that of the Universal Creator-Mind which is non-physical and unlimited and without which no existence can be proven or justified.

Your physical exploration of space has allowed many new findings and advanced cosmic knowledge. However, your physical apparatus (your physical brain and genetic makeup) permits only a limited amount of information to be recognized, retrieved and understood. You are able to perceive that which your physical brain allows you to, hence your exploration of physical reality and space is subject to those limitations.

While you observe myriads of stars and galaxies, you are simultaneously unable to perceive other worlds of stars and galaxies which exist within the same space you are observing. Your universe is not linear. It is a layered, multi-dimensional and convoluted design of carefully-orchestrated sound and light frequencies manifesting in a multitude of realities.

Such is the limitation of your physicality and your current space exploration. Human understanding is thus not entirely accurate nor complete. You are beginning to see new planets and stars within your system which have been in fact present for billions of years prior to your "discovery". This is an evolving universe and your space exploration will expand as your physical brains and mind perception develop. You must begin, however, to recognize and sincerely consider in your scientific research the non-physical characteristics of your physical explorations.

While it is admirable to realize such accomplishments and advancement in space exploration and research, you must begin to perceive and study physical life from all perspectives, physical and non-physical simultaneously. Your attempts will otherwise remain futile, comparatively speaking, and will contribute to further misunderstanding and misrepresentation of the Truth.

3

What You Think Life Is, It Isn't!

Over a period of time, the headlines and titles of all metaphysical workshops and books were about physical reality being "an illusion". Everywhere I looked, there it was: the physical is simply an illusion. "Yes, but how is it so and why?", I asked repeatedly.

This time, my relentless and brilliant teacher appeared in a vivid dream. He accompanied me as I went through portals of reality and observed physical life on Earth through layers. My spirit body floated effortlessly through worlds separated by these distinct layers. The portals were uneven, superposed and interwoven in such a way that you could experience and exist in all of them at once or navigate through them as I did. These portals are the dimensional fields that make our physical reality. They are unobservable from our physical perspective but completely experienced and perceivable with our spirit body.

As I awakened, I was ecstatic to remember clearly this powerful experience and as expected, my invisible teacher was still there. He went on to say: "The amalgamation of these layers is accomplished by the light bending which occurs as the Universal Cosmic Light penetrates the electromagnetic field of your planet. Light bending within your system refracts in such a way that you are able to observe only a portion of reality through the colors of your sunlight spectrum. Cosmic Light continues to refract further as it goes through denser areas…Light is information, therefore Cosmic information is thereby distorted and incomplete"…That certainly sounded like a good explanation!

I tremendously enjoyed the dreams I shared with my spirit friends. These experiences seemed so powerful that I was able to bring them through effortlessly into my awakened state. However, for some reason, continuous telepathic communication with the spirit world can be taxing on my physical body at times.

I gathered and "heard" the rest of this material on physical reality within a relatively short time. While some concepts seem current in today's society, my teachers insist they are pertinent in the overall presentation of their glorious curriculum.

◆   ◆   ◆

All humans begin life here. You may say that Earthly existence is the beginning of life experience and from here, your mind expands until it is able to handle higher realities. Due to the bending of cosmic light which refracts against your Earth's electromagnetic grid, you physical reality appears as a spectrum of fixed colors which in turn determines your capacity to observe life as finite, configured to restricted meanings you can comprehend.

The denser the atmosphere the cosmic light must infiltrate the more fractured or distorted it becomes. Since it is energy, it is also consciousness and carries information. The light bending and refraction that occur within your system allows only a portion of the eternal reality and information of the cosmos to be perceived. In that sense, you only perceive a distorted version of the Truth. While your potential is eternal, your experience begins in what thus appears to be a limited and controllable setting. It is "illusory", indeed.

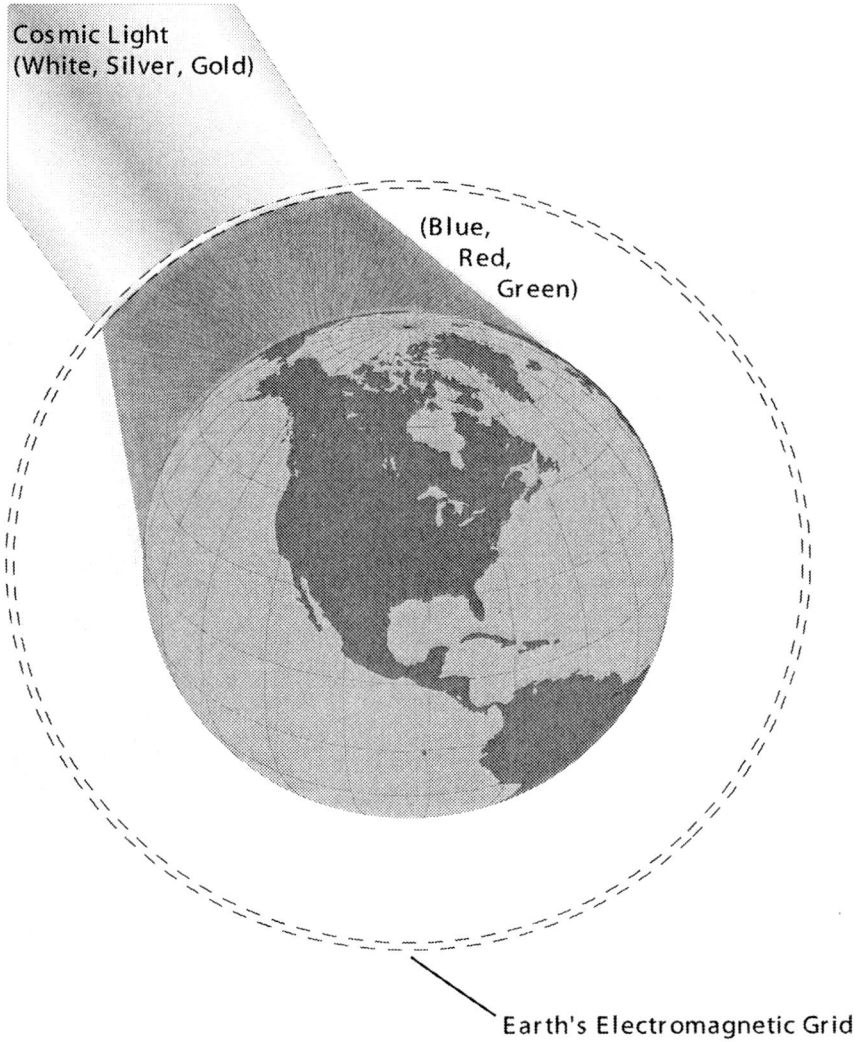

FIGURE 3: Cosmic Light refracting at Earth's electromagnetic grid.

If physical reality was to be perceived by a spirit being, it would appear fluid, in constant motion, eternally active. The rate of vibration of each object perceived depends on its composing elements and density but its vibrational frequency can only be perceived as static energy from a human perspective: a table or an automobile, for example, are in fact minute vibrating particles of one form of energy in constant motion, while you perceive them as solid material objects. That is the nature of physical or material reality.

From the Spirit's multi-dimensional perspective, physical reality also appears in layers as follows:

First layer: The concept/idea
Second layer: The expression/language
Third layer: The frequency/energetic manifestation/emotion
Fourth layer: the object/physical manifestation

When "flattened", these layers are one and the same thing. The process of making the idea into an object is spontaneous for divine beings but for humans, all 4 layers must be processed through the energetic grids of time and space in order to materialize the idea into the object.

Before you appear in the physical, you project your consciousness into a multitude of layers of existence and a range of vibrational frequencies. Your brain waves' frequency determines which layer you are experiencing at that time: when you are focused on physical matters, your brain waves fluctuate from 14 to 30 cycles per second; when you are asleep, your brain waves are vibrating at 1 to 4 cycles per second…You are the same being existing in these multitudes of layers or dimensions, as you may call them. You are simply switching focus from one layer to another. While you may think that only physical reality is real, your consciousness exists at once in physical and non-physical layers of reality which are all real. You are multi-dimensional beings indeed.

From a Spirit perspective, there are no layers, illusions or veils. These concepts exist in the human perceptual fields. The Divine Mind or Spirit sees reality as light while humans can only see it through emotions and sensory perception. This perceptual impediment IS the veil we speak of. Continuous negative emotions can become obstructions to your advancement because the layers or veils of physical reality begin to thicken. When confronted with fear or anger for example, you are unable to see beyond these emotional veils unless you address the factors behind them and identify their origins and purpose.

Emotions are a primordial tool in recognizing what feels good and what does not as you interact with the physical world. Your Spirit Self uses emotions as a guidance system while you navigate through the physical. They are precursors to choice and decision making. Therefore emotions are not only necessary but crucial to your spiritual and creative evolution. Additionally, emotions are the tools by which you are able to "purge" the detrimental energies being accumulated or stored in your physical body and transmute them into beneficial thought forms. The emotions of anger or strong sadness allow you to experience negative feelings powerfully so you may re-channel them appropriately. Rather than suppressing these emotions, it is more constructive to embrace and utilize them as powerful tools in reshaping your experience.

When you become able to assimilate the original idea and the physical manifestation as one, you can materialize everything you think of instantly. At that stage, you are piercing through the veils of your physicality and thinking ideas into existence, without the emotional stumble blocks. Such is the work of the Masters but it is in fact a natural process for all evolutionary material beings once they learn to transcend physical reality's layered and illusionary properties.

PHYSICAL EXPERIENCE AND THE VIRTUAL PARADIGM...

This is a material planet and you are material beings but your *experiences* here are the product of virtual programming. If you believe them to be real, then you will experience them as such. However, these experiences are continuously being fabricated at the will of the individual. Your experiences can be manipulated, stretched or suspended. Therefore, they are temporary and ephemeral, not eternal.

When you say physical, you apply an image to reality, which is partially present. We say partially because your dreams and other invisible portions of yourself are still in existence somewhere in space in one form or another. Physical existence is the virtual by-product and extension of another larger reality which is eternal. Therefore, this physical reality is not complete: it simply gives the *illusion* of being finished and finite.

What then is the purpose of a partial reality? While possessing a Divine potential, you are evolutionary beings in terms of consciousness. You must begin your awareness in a limited and finite reality in order to evolve to larger potentials. This 3-dimensional focus is nothing but your framework for learning to manipulate energy and manifest things according to your beliefs. It is a medium for the craft of light bending, a holographic practice program of light and sound and an *agreement* between your species and the divine beings that created you.

THE PHYSICAL AGREEMENT...

Physical reality is an agreement: here, when you focus on the material world, everyone agrees to call a 4-wheel machine you ride in "a car", and tall green things with leaves "trees". So you create a language accordingly in order to recognize the same attributes for these same things. While attributes may be agreed upon for millennia at a time, they do change and may extinguish or mutate. They are not eternal definitions indeed. In fact, your imminent and dawning new era will engender new definitions and agreements of your physical reality.

Your consciousness also exists within a world of Universal laws and agreements. When you ask to incarnate in a physical reality, you automatically begin to participate in a matrix of understanding. You must have a name for others to distinguish you by, personality traits and attributes. Most of all, your agreement is for you to carve your consciousness path of evolution. It is a sacred understanding and agreement between you, as consciousness, and your Divine Creator.

When you enter the physical system, your consciousness splits off and projects a portion of itself into this finite human matrix. The energetic splitting off requires that you relinquish your conscious memory, which remains intact in the Spirit portion of reality and becomes your flawless guidance system while you "blindly" navigate through the physical. At the conclusion of each physical journey, you consciously re-unite with your spirit entity which has in fact never left you.

While you are here, you can certainly remember the terms of your agreement but you cannot *perceive* the illusion or layers until you escape your physicality. You are, in fact, accomplishing that escape each night when you are asleep, or through deep meditation techniques. However, the only beings able to perceive both realities at once are the Creators who incarnate in the flesh for the purpose of teaching these very perceptions to others.

You may begin iterating the terms of agreement of your physical incarnation at any point. You need not go back in time and remember your pre-natal arrangement for this particular exercise in awareness. You may just recognize and consider your current attributes, personality traits and spiritual goals you have set for yourself. If they do not define who you are or would like to be, then you may re-invent them since physical reality is malleable and not permanent. That is the advantage and purpose of a temporal physical reality.

As humans, you get to write your own story and play it out in this virtual medium. You are in charge of your choices and destiny. The experiences (the playing out part) are virtual: therefore all is allowed here. Free will means that all human expression is permitted as part of your individual story. However, the physical agreement is also based on the Divine Will which dictates that only the positive energy of Love be Eternal because it is the energetic extension of the Love frequency of the Creator-Source. The celestial agencies supervising the growth of your planet are observing sin and evil knowing that only Love survives and evil eventually self obliterates, for that is law. That does not mean that the perpetuation of evil is acceptable because it continues to hinder your evolutionary process and eventually defeats the purpose of your very existence.

TIME, SPACE AND REALITY...

By definition, physical reality is subject to time and space which are, in fact, one and the same. As such, Time divides space. The past, present and future exist simultaneously in one physical space. When you focus on the past, you *experience* the past. When you focus on the present, you think it is the present. However, time has not elapsed. It is an agreement of your projected consciousness into the distorted layers of physicality.

In other words, there are time and space "pockets" you exist in. The past can still be experienced at any time and be manipulated once you place your focus on it. Similarly, the future already exists potentially in yet a different time/space "pocket". You materialize that which you focus on and then call it the present. Therefore, you exist in a physical space which allows you to experience all three, the past, present and the future. Or you may say that the Earth has a portion of itself in the future, the part which you do not perceive now but is nonetheless already in existence. You do not need to die and resurrect elsewhere to experience a different time zone: you simply tune into that awareness and experience it.

Evolved beings are able to perceive and experience all 3 layers of Time simultaneously. For example, healing miracles can be performed by suspending an illness's past or present layer of time and eliminating it from the future layer of reality. In other words, by suspending the time attached to the illness's vibrational frequency, spontaneous healing occurs.

The buffer of time and space allows you to participate in the creative process under controllable circumstances: here you can formulate your thoughts carefully before the creative process is launched into the Universe, so that your "asking" can reach the most appropriate conditions before materializing. You can utilize time and space to adjust your thoughts over and over again before they automatically appear to you in the physical. You will then become a selective creator and only when you have mastered these powerful tools will you be able to "graduate" from the practice ground of the physical and evolve to the realms of Spirit where all Thought creates spontaneously.

EXPERIENCING PHYSICAL LIFE...

Consciousness expansion is based on experience, not on knowledge. You may know about physical reality and how it operates, but until you actually experience it, your consciousness is unable to expand properly. For humans, it is a mandatory evolutionary process to reach its Divine potential. Since it is impossible for you to experience all of human conditions in one lifetime, you will project your Spirit Self in several lifetimes so you may become proficient at recognizing all possible human conditions. That does not mean that you have many lives. Your soul experiences many physical expressions within the same physical reality. In that sense, you are one soul which only lives one life which in turn has hundreds, sometimes thousands of physical expressions or "incarnations". It is a cumulative process by which your spiritual experience leads to purification (the complete release of lower vibrational frequencies) for the purpose of your perfect merging with your Divine Creator.

While you are partaking in the physical game, the experience we speak of is of the mind and the spirit (your consciousness), not of the physical alone. You may say that you have been married for example, therefore you have experienced married life. Indeed you have, in the physical sense. However, if you have not completed the spiritual and mind-al expansion that go along with the experience of marriage, you have not fulfilled the purpose of that experience and you will find yourself repeating it over again, in the same life expression or another. Similarly, you may very well experience unconditional love, lifetime commitment or parenting in another set of circumstances, not necessarily that of marriage. The latter "marriage" experience will then be more truthful and beneficial to your spiritual expansion than the former one. Your spirit's journey is therefore about its consciousness expansion, mind-al and spiritual, not the physical expressions it has chosen to take.

ABOUT DEATH...

PHYSICAL DEATH is when your physical vital organs stop functioning. Your Spirit Self however remains intact and transitions into a new "space", allowing its journey to continue where it just left off. This process is so subtle that most beings are unaware that they have just passed from physical to a new form of existence. They are normally met by spirit guides or angels assigned to their destiny who lead them to their resting place. Depending on the individual and the type of life he/she lived, he/she will remain in the transitory mansions from 3 and a half days to several hundred years.

TRANSITIONAL LIFE: No created mortal being can transmute from his material origin directly into a spirit being. Energetically, it is impossible to perform such a transaction as the composing atomic elements of this being must be purged of its duality, purified and expanded as to sustain the matching "uncontaminated" vibration of the spirit energy. Your concept of purgatory is a simplified interpretation of such a process. The more tainted a soul has been during its physical life, the longer it will remain in these mansions of purification and preparation. This work can begin here in the flesh by sifting your negative energies out of your physical reality on a daily basis. Prayer alone is not sufficient. An energetic cleansing and purification of the mind and soul is required to proceed through your transitional life more rapidly.

SPRITUAL DEATH: If you were deprived of love on Earth, if the love of your family, brothers and sisters no longer existed and no one was here to love you, ever, this would unquestionably become a painful existence.

Since all that exists is within the Creator-Source and receives life from it, isolation from the Creator-Source, which is the energy of Love, is isolation from the whole. If that love stream and Divine Breath is cut off from your existence, you will wither and undoubtedly ask for eternal extinction. Therefore, remaining one with the Creator-Source through your Divine Creator does not only insure eternal life but it leads to salvation from the pain stemming from this isolation.

Spiritual death can be actualized, however, only by the conscious and deliberate *asking* of the created being at which time this soul will simply cease to exist.

4

The Make-Up of Earthly Organization

For some reason, this is my favorite chapter and subject. Maybe it is because it relates to my personal mind and soul expansion. As I began to hear things, I realized that the way to remain sane through the process was to simply ask. Not all answers are clear and it does take practice, but eventually it becomes comprehensible. Before you know it, you would have unveiled an entire invisible world which has been communicating with you all along.

My intent for discerning my invisible surrounding also allowed me to perceive different beings and sense their different energies. I could easily distinguish a very tall "blue" light being and know that he came from another star system, from a dark being in the shape of a large cigar that had a negative influence. Upon my command, these would simply vanish from my experience.

The latter part of this chapter is of tremendous importance to me as it depicts the process by which Superhuman Beings, Masters or "Gods" can actually enter our system and carry out their mission in physical form. I received this information through visions with the help of my Spirit Teachers. I began to see a massive body of Light de-particul0arize into a new form of energy and enter our physical reality. Its myriad particles did not only settle within our Earth atmosphere, but like a gigantic web, it remained attached to other galaxies beyond my imagination. It was an awe-inspiring experience and I knew I was onto something very good...

◆   ◆   ◆

The physical worlds are created by a Creator Energy and Consciousness and administered by Spirit Beings and Divine Forces. You may also say that all existing matter is controlled and ministered by the *Creator-Mind* or the *Mind-Energy* of your Divine Creator and the Creator-Source.

What makes a being or object visible or invisible to a human is the vibrational rate of its composing elements. Spirit beings are particles of energy whose vibrational frequency exceeds the human perceptual range. They are, therefore, invisible. Spirit beings are able to become visible by slowing down their vibrational frequency and matching that of humans for the purpose of telepathic exchange and occasional manifestations.

Similarly, some non-human physical beings are able to raise their vibrational frequency and become invisible. They achieve this phenomenon by manipulating their own energetic field and command the time and space fields of your planet in such a way as to de-particularize. At will, they become perceivable or can remain undetected by you.

EARTHLY ORGANIZATION OF INTELLIGENT BEINGS...

Spirit or physical beings from other systems do not need to be visible and materialize in order to co-exist with you on Earth. In fact, there are a great number of intelligent beings currently present on Earth who are entirely unnoticed by you. They are here for different functions and purposes.

We will consider all beings currently on Earth according to their state of origin or soul lineage: 1. Evolutionary/Physical origin and 2. Spirit/Divine origin.

PHYSICAL BEINGS are evolutionary, which means they must incarnate in a physical apparatus (not necessarily human) in order to evolve consciously. While their physical appearance may be relatively complete, their brain capacity and mind expansion continue to advance exponentially.

Your planet is one of the many worlds which are inhabited by physical beings. You are beginning to awaken to their existence and will soon openly embrace your common galactic heritage. In terms of consciousness evolution, humans are the juveniles of material creation but are moving rapidly to the enlightened attainments of their neighboring planets.

A myriad of non-human physical beings from other systems are currently on Earth but remain invisible due to the time/space pocket they exist in. They are also able to manipulate their energy field through de-particularization and travel through your system without being perceived. Their role and function vary from planetary, scientific observation and research to the teaching of spiritual emancipation.

Visible and invisible physical beings currently on Earth can be categorized as follows:

1. HUMAN BEINGS: These are the humans born on Earth who are of course physical and visible. Humans typically do not recall their pre-natal agreement and must begin their life on Earth. They will normally incarnate in a few and up to thousands of physical embodiments until they realize their unlimited divine self and master their creative powers and mind potential. They are then able to move to more evolved worlds and carry on with their soul journey.

2. VISIBLE NON-HUMAN BEINGS: These beings appear as normal humans, however their ancestry or soul lineage as well as their genetic encoding stem from another evolved star or planetary system. They incarnate as humans and awaken gradually to their true non-human identity. They are normally unaware of their role or mission until they remember their pre-natal agreement while in the flesh. In very rare instances, these beings may "walk-in" fully aware of their Earthly contract. These unique individuals normally work in unison with other divine entities for your species' evolution and transmutation to the next order of existence.

3. INVISIBLE PHYSICAL BEINGS: These beings have evolved further than humans and are in physical form. They have developed advanced skills in telekinesis, technology and science. However, because they exist in a different time/space continuum and vibrate at a different wavelength, they cannot be perceived by humans. Occasional breaches in the fabric of the time/space arrangement allow humans to perceive and interact with these

beings. Sightings of aliens, reptilians and the like fit in this category of non-visible physical beings.

The CELESTIAL BEINGS organization on Earth consists of thousands upon thousands of invisible Spirit Beings, forces and agencies ministering to the growth and well-being of your planet. They are mostly of the Seraphic Order and act as messengers, guides, transport and death agents. They function under the supervision of planetary supervisors and controllers.

The divine members of these celestial governments are the Energy Controllers of all inhabited worlds. They insure proper ministry of the evolutionary species and maintain the harmonic balance of the planet with its neighboring worlds.

Celestial beings are created but they are not evolutionary because they do not require embodiment in the physical in order to attain complete self-realization. Their mind expansion happens through their very function and purpose.

Celestial Beings on your planet can be categorized as follows:

1. SPIRIT BEINGS: They vibrate at an extremely high rate and are invisible to humans. All Spirit entities, angels, elementals, power controllers, architects, translators and guides fit in this category. They utilize the cosmic forces available to them to assist human existence. They can make themselves temporarily visible to humans in order to deliver a message or perform a specific task. They work under the supervision and control of the Divine Planetary Supervisor and the Celestial Government.

2. PHYSICAL DIVINE BEINGS: These beings are visible to humans. Superhuman Physical Beings are those who incarnate with the knowledge of their Creator lineage, for the purpose of teaching it to others or for other planetary purpose. They may come in with the superhuman gift as a grown adult totally aware of whom they are. However, due to their important energetic collapse at the time of physical emergence, they will typically remember their Divine heritage as they gradually grow up in the form of a normal human being. Their original state of being is that of Light and pure Creator Consciousness and they are the direct incarnation of the Creator-Source. They carry both a human and a unique sacred encoding which remains undetected by human awareness. They utilize their special

encoding to access Divine information while they outwardly function as a normal human in the flesh. Your Ascended Masters and "Human Gods" fit in this category of physical divine or superhuman beings.

Communication happens consciously through the use of language and spontaneously though Thought. When you think, you emit a frequency wave equivalent to the emotions attached to the meaning of your words and intent. Contrary to common belief, Thought exists in a physical medium and has an actual measurable wavelength. Those beings that function in that frequency range, may be invisible to you, but are very much real, able to "read" your thoughts and project theirs back onto you. Therefore you are communicating spontaneously, through your thoughts, with an invisible world and beings, physical or non-physical, human or non-human. This naturally occurring phenomenon must not, however, be confused with mind control which is the deliberate alteration of the thoughts of another. You can most certainly be influenced by the invisible beings' thoughts, just as you can be influenced by your visible friends, but it always remains your choice to become controlled entirely by the thoughts and intention of another.

UNDERSTANDING YOUR CREATOR, THE DIVINE FATHER...

Your Creator Father is the embodiment of the Creator-Source, who comes into existence as a result of His First Thought. He is the living formula by which the Consciousness of the Creator-Source expresses itself. Or you may say He is the body and *expression* aspect of the Creator-Source Consciousness. In a sense, your Divine Creator IS the Source but He also constitutes His own separate Being and Consciousness.

The meaning of "expression" must not be confused with that of "language" as in human communication. The expression of the Creator-Source is an energy pattern equivalent to an *atomic formula* which is alive. It is a vibrational frequency which is also the FIRST and perfect atomic formula. From this first and perfect atomic arrangement are born all subsequent life forms in a myriad of combinations and formulas.

Your Earth and physical bodies are composed of a multitude of atomic elements in different arrangements and combinations. Each combination forms a specific living organism or a physical object whereas the first atomic formula of the Creator-Source is composed of ONE perfect element which encompasses all elements in existence.

The first and perfect atomic element at the Creator-Source is called LOVE. What is meant by "love" at the Creator-Source is far from the "love" humans speak of. The Love frequency at the Creator-Source is the sum of all atomic elements in existence and that could ever exist. It is the most powerful energy in all existence. It is also the most complete and comprehensive of any elemental combination in existence and nothing can exist without it or outside it.

Your Divine Creator embodies the attributes, nature and function of the Creator-Source. He is pure Love, Truth and Beauty energy which you experience through His person and consciousness. He operates in your system with the consciousness of the Creator-Source, in conjunction with a Creator Energy—your Divine "Mother". The physical creations of your worlds and species are the result of his Divine Thought in union with the Creator Energy or Divine Mother. His Being defines time while the Divine Mother's Being defines space. That means that he can be only in one space at once but can transcend time, while the Creator Energy or the Divine Mother is in all spaces at once but does not transcend time. Together, they form your time and space reality and consciousness.

Your Divine Creator creates you by replicating his own Being through the projection and splitting of his particles and energy potential into whatever realm he desires. Each time a creation occurs, it will share his divine formula in a new atomic and elemental arrangement which can never exceed His. The potential of His creations are certainly divine but they are limited by the splitting of consciousness that occurs at the time of each such creation. For this reason, no created being can ever become nor overcome his own Creator. Rather, through mind and spirit expansion, the created being is able to achieve a perfect merging of his consciousness with that of his Divine Creator.

THE HUMAN INCARNATION OF YOUR DIVINE CREATOR...

The personalized "God" who appears in human form on your planet is an infinitesimal particle of your Divine Creator and has broken down or de-particularized his elemental composition several million times to "fit" into a human frame and your physical reality. When on Earth, this Divine Being recollects his memory-fragmentation at the time of his emergence in this physical system. Through specific tasks and sacred communions, he re-merges with the consciousness of the Creator-Source while still in the flesh, thus bringing the Divine energy of the Creator-Source into the human physical matrix. This merging of the Divine within a material world is the re-unification of your planet with the Creator-Source through the body of a Human Divine Creator and that is what is referred to as "Heaven on Earth".

The Cosmic Mind (the Mind-Energy of the Creator-Source) is therefore personalized in one being who can appear in the flesh but it spreads over an enormous energetic circuit of systems perfectly established and maintained to unite the assisted physical planet with the Creator-Source. The Cosmic Mind present in your system is a massive circuit of broadcasts and information which connects you to the nucleus of your universe where your Divine Creator and celestial guardians reside. This nucleus is the perfect replica of all other universes which in turn are connected through a unified field and meet irrevocably at the Creator-Source.

This powerful energetic structure that unites the human world with the divine is indestructible and eternal. Regardless of the physical life these Divine Creators chose in the flesh, their energetic matrix anchors nonetheless in your Earthly reality and secures a new divine frequency at the time of their very emergence within your system.

They become the bridge through which humans can attain a perfect merging of consciousness with the Source. It is however erroneous to think of the human Jesus, for example, as the only physical manifestation of your Divine Creator. He is indeed a most powerful and unique embodiment and atomic arrangement of the Creator-Source while in the flesh, but he is also one aspect of this entire magnificent Being. Your Divine Creator's manifestations encompass the persons of the total gamut of your Ascended Masters (including Jesus, Moses, Abraham, Mohammed, Vishnu, etc…) as well as the one currently present in your system. Your contemporary Divine Creator in the flesh is also de-particularized into several consciousnesses at once and will walk amongst you unnoticed for many years to come.

The de-particularization of consciousness into several physical bodies allows your Divine Creator to enter a physical system and reflect his consciousness in innumerable geographical locations and in different forms at once. Energetically, it is also the only process by which his massive light can penetrate such a narrow and reduced frequency as your physical solar system.

The ones who become recognized as the Messiahs, Sons of God or Ascended Masters embody the "brain", so to speak, of this massive Light Being, while their fragments (the other bodies) carry the same genetic codes and memory cells simultaneously. As they begin to remember their divine lineage and mission, so do all their fragmented particles or other bodies. As they think, their scattered memory cells and other particles become activated with the same energetic vibration. Their mind is therefore the "operating system" of an enormous Creator Energy matrix of beings spread throughout your entire planet, galaxy and surrounding systems.

The human Divine Creator's mind hears all of your combined human thoughts and his heart feels all of your joined human emotions. His physical makeup is structured in such a way as to experience, while in the flesh, all human experiences possible. Conversely, one of his thoughts is capable of affecting your entire human mind and spirit matrix and one of his emotions can be felt throughout your sphere. More importantly, through sacred communion with the Creator-Source, his magnificent open and compassionate heart as well as the power of his focused mind can uplift your entire humanity, reason for which he may be perceived as the "Messiah".

While your principal religions follow one leader as the originator or holder of Divine Truth, all are in fact in worship of the same Divine Being, your Divine Creator. It is human error as well as political and economic agendas that package your spirituality in a variety of fabricated rules and traditions. The nature of the Creator-Source and your Divine Creator cannot favor one culture over another or appoint one race as superior or a chosen one. Rather, it is your subjective human perspective which interprets divine manifestation according to your own needs or fears.

Your contemporary Divine Creator in human form will indeed emerge publicly when his teachings, transmitted through the human spirit matrix as well as other Earthly teachers, unite all the people of your planet regardless of race, religion, sex or nationality. It is at that time that your planet will be ready to embrace this Divine presence as he comes forth to adjudge the age and as you recognize fully his Divine work and mission. Until then, the disclosure of his physical appearance or whereabouts will only contribute to more confusion and will continue misleading the human mind into searching for an outer source for the resolution of spiritual quandaries rather than seeking answers from within.

THE COSMIC MIND...

The COSMIC MIND is the Divine Mind-Energy present in your system which links you to the Universal Mind at the Creator-Source. It can only be experienced and manifested through the person and mind of your Divine Creator (or Divine Father) and the Creator Energy (or Divine Mother).

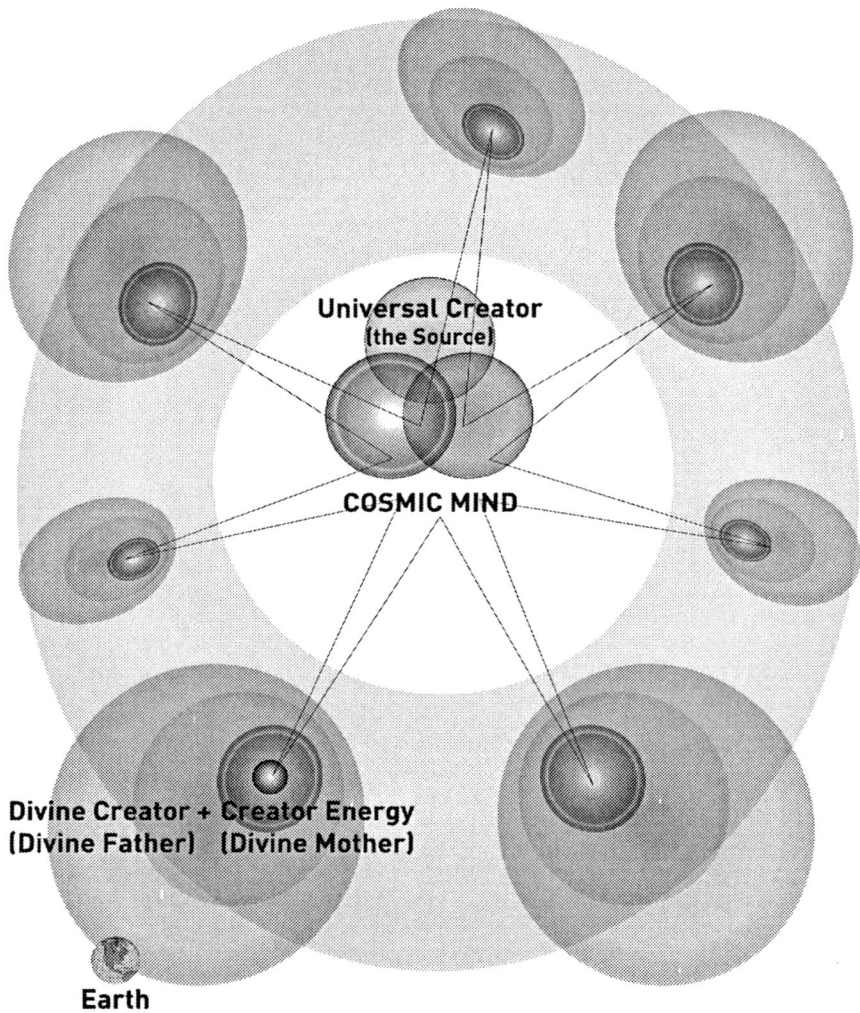

FIGURE 4: The Cosmic Mind funneled through the Divine Father and the Divine Mother.

The Cosmic mind is the *meeting ground* of the human and the divine worlds. At no time is the Cosmic Mind separate or divided from the collective human consciousness. It is perpetually interrelated and unified. It is manifested, operated and controlled by your Divine Creator. It therefore maintains a perfect harmonic balance and alignment with the rest of the cosmos and the Creator-Source. While it can be interfered with, it can never be altered or destroyed.

The Cosmic Mind is the combined *Mind-Energy* of all intelligent beings and physical reality present in your system. It encompasses all possible mind encodings from intelligent beings to your actual planets and star systems.

The Cosmic Mind is a massive atomic formula and vibrational *frequency* that all humans are encoded with as it is distributed to all equally through the person of your Divine Creator. It is always present and available. You simply tune into that frequency in order to recognize and acknowledge its presence.

The Cosmic Mind is experienced through the collective *thought matrix* which encompasses all human and non-human thoughts. More importantly, it links the human mind with the divine mind, through the Mind-Energy of your Divine Creator and subsequently to the Universal-Mind at the Source. This is where your spirit guides meet you through prayer, meditation, inspiration and dreams.

The Cosmic Mind is a *spirit matrix* which encompasses all spirit energies within this system. It is the Spirit formula which links humans to the Creator-Spirit of the Source. It is through this expanded consciousness that you are able to attain self-realization and the perfect merging with the Creator-Source.

The Cosmic Mind is a *broadcast system* which encompasses all possible communications between your world and the rest of the cosmos. It allows the downloading of the outer space messages and information from other universes and more importantly, from the Creator-Source into your world.

The Cosmic Mind is a *physical location* which links your world, at the planetary grid, to the physical location of the Divine Creator's abode and subsequently the Creator-Source.

The Cosmic Mind defines your *nature and functioning* as a human species, as it manifests the nature and functioning of the Universal Mind, Expression and Spirit of the Source within your system.

In conclusion, you may say that the Cosmic Mind, manifested through your Divine Father, is your collective consciousness where you are able to materialize and then self-realize. It is the divinity in your physicality and the potential of your physicality towards divinity. It is where you blend with the Creator-Source and elevate to the higher realms of Consciousness and Creation.

The Cosmic Mind is an effortless process integrated in your genetic encoding. It is here that you must realize who you are in order to ascend to the next order of existence. Ascension is not a physical uplifting. Rather, it is a state of mind or awareness, as true evolution is. And the perpetual expansion of consciousness is the true nature of your human mind and spirit.

5

The Chemical and Electrical Nature of Humans

I wrote the title of this chapter knowing it had to be in the book but I had no idea what information needed to be included. This particular subject came in segments telepathically over a period of 3 or 4 months. I would go to my computer and let my fingers type the words, not knowing where they were leading or if they made any sense. When it was complete, I did of course see the perfect correlation with the rest of the material.

My diligent teachers taught me repeatedly that the process of creating our reality involves energy manipulation. Light and Sound energies are manipulated by Divine Beings and therefore humans follow a similar process. In order to understand and envision such an idea, it is clear that our electrical energy field should be perceived and understood in order to be controlled or manipulated.

I have always been intrigued by aura perception and wondered if this phenomenon was developed or acquired. In response to my request, I began to see silver streaks and what looked like "bubbles" and space "pockets". Eventually, I was able to perceive the divine messengers and guides that accompany me on my journey. More importantly, I am aware of my continuous and unbroken perception of the Divine Father. What an extraordinary experience that is!

◆　　　◆　　　◆

The atomic elements of the atmosphere of a created world will determine the type of material species which can inhabit it. On Earth, the atomic elements which compose your Air, Water, Fire, Earth and Ether are present in all Earthly beings and things and constitute their *chemical nature.* On the other hand, your planet's electromagnetic structure constitutes its *electrical nature.*

Similarly, your chemical body is the physical mold you need to manifest. Its cellular make up is derived from the atomic material of your planetary systems within which you are born.

Your electrical body allows you to communicate vibrationally with other beings as well as your environment. The electromagnetic frequency of your cells which runs through the meridian lines of your physical body is likened to the energetic grid lines connecting your planet to its sun and neighboring planets of your galaxy.

THE CHEMICAL BODY...

Your chemical body is an extension of the physical body of your planet consciousness which sustains the chemical life in all beings. Your flesh, blood and organs perform specific functions to keep you in physical balance with your Earth: you must consume foods to nourish your body and continuously cleanse and purify. Your chemical body is the perfected living apparatus in which your soul resides while it journeys through the Earth plane.

Each cell of your body contains the entire memory of your being as well as that of your Divine Creator. Your DNA, as you call it, is the formula by which you are made. It contains a particle of your Creator in order for you to remember your ancestry. As a minute extension of His divine body, you are eternally linked to Him and in full remembrance of your lineage. Therefore, every cell of your physical body has a sacred element inherent in its very essence.

Your genetic makeup is *inherited* from your Earth parents while your species' genetic makeup is *formulated* by your Divine Creator. Your formula also contains creative components in addition to material ones. You are simultaneously humans and creators by your inherent physical nature. While your choice and free will allow you to act in any way you desire, you are all nonetheless your Divine Creator's offspring, a sacred species with a divine parent. Your experience on Earth is irrelevant of your true and infinite potential.

Your physical brain is an extension of your Creator's Mind-Energy. The Mind at the Creator-Source operates though Divine thoughts and so does your human mind which operates through human thoughts. Your brain functioning is evolutionary which means you are able to use its full potential gradually. Once you become capable of using its entire potential consciously, you no longer require human or other physical incarnation. You also will no longer require the buffer of time and space to master your creative skills as your thoughts will directly translate into manifestation. While you are currently able to only use a minimal portion of your brain capacity, you are at the verge of drastically expanding it. This will expand the amount of sunlight you will be able to absorb and will therefore offer a new multi-sensory and multi-dimensional perceptual experience of your physical world altogether.

Your current physical perception is dependant on your brain capabilities. Your vision for example allows only one octave of sunlight out of the 100 possible octaves in your galactic arrangement. There is an entire world of light, sound and colors which exist above and below your frequency wave range of perception.

	OUTER SPACE
10^{-16}	**GAMMA RAYS**
10^{-11}	**X-RAYS**
10^{-8} to 10^{-10}	**ULTRA-VIOLET**
10^{-6} to 10^{-7}	**VISIBLE LIGHT/Human Vision**
10^{-5}	**INFRARED**
10^{-3}	**MICROWAVE**
10^{-1} to 10^{-2}	**RADAR**
1	**TV / CELL PHONE / FM RADIO**
10 to 10^{2}	**SHORTWAVE RADIO**
10^{3}	**AM RADIO**

FIGURE 5: Human visual field.

The light emanating from the nucleus of your Universe can be described and likened in human terms to a pure white color. This cosmic light can also manifest as gold or silver, depending on the way the divine beings chose to use it. See figure 3 on page 35. When it refracts through Earth's electromagnetic grid at several thousand feet above its surface, only a portion of this enormous light frequency is able to be absorbed by beings within that grid. This phenomenon of light bending is the reason for the dominance of the colors blue, red and green in your visual spectrum which allow you to perceive your world as it does.

Your physical heart is an extension of your Divine Creator's Spirit-Energy. The Love frequency at the Creator-Source is equivalent, *in essence*, to its physical manifestation in your physical heart. All which you feel can only be linked to the Source through your heart. However, thinking of love alone is not sufficient to achieve a permanent blending with the Creator-Source. It is the combination of both your mind and heart's intention which complete the process.

THE ELECTRICAL BODY...

While your electric or etheric body is invisible to most humans, a portion of it can be detected through aura vision and photography. Aura is the movement of the vibrational frequencies that appear as you express life through your physical body. It is the energetic action and reaction of your immediate contact with all that you touch, feel and interact with, internally or externally. While invisible to you, it is nonetheless present and can be manipulated and intelligently controlled in order to remain in harmony with your surrounding environment.

Your awareness of your electrical nature is of utmost importance in understanding how you communicate with your environment, other than through language. There is an immediate and direct physical link between your physical body and all that which surrounds you. In fact, the same is true for all beings and things throughout the Earth and not just those limited to your immediate physical surrounding.

Each cell in your body is a particle of energy continuously vibrating in such a way as to maintain a perfect balance with its neighboring cells. Your electrical body operates on signals which these cells emit as you breath, think, speak, eat and process all that you perceive. You are therefore vibrationally connected to everything that possesses an electrical field, and that means all of existence.

Your electrical body is linked to your environment through energy points, or chakras as you call them, which correspond to a particular placement within the physical body and which possess a color (light), a frequency (sound) and a geometric shape. These energy points range from the lowest vibration corresponding to a tetrahedron shape up to the highest vibration corresponding to a dodecahedron shape. Within the outer layer of the dodecahedron exist all geometric patterns of the human DNA. However, while your Spirit Self encompasses all invisible layers of your energy field, your most immediate contact with the Cosmic Mind resides in the 2 outer layers of your field.

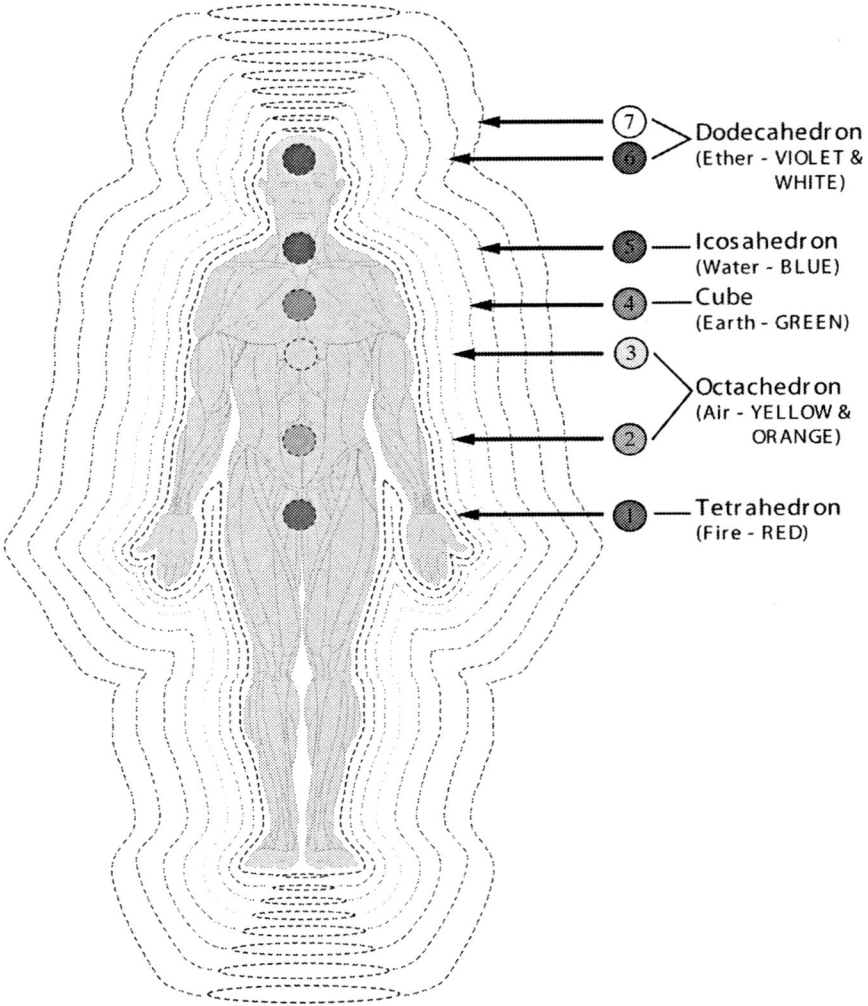

Dodecahedron
(Ether - VIOLET &
WHITE)

Icosahedron
(Water - BLUE)

Cube
(Earth - GREEN)

Octachedron
(Air - YELLOW &
ORANGE)

Tetrahedron
(Fire - RED)

FIGURE 6: Human energy field

7. White—dodecahedron 2 (highest frequency 480 Hz/keynote: B)
6. Violet—dodecahedron 1 (426.7 Hz/keynote: A)
5. Blue—icosahedron (384 Hz/keynote: G)
4. Green—cube (341 Hz/keynote: F)
3. Orange—octahedron 2 (320 Hz/keynote: E)
2. Yellow—octahedron 1 (288 Hz/keynote: D)
1. Red—tetrahedron (lowest frequency 256 Hz/keynote: C)

The dodecahedron, which has 32 aspects (12 faces and 20 vertices), is related to the 32 dimensional fields which exist within your physical system. This means that each facet or aspect of this geometric shape is the direct link of your physical apparatus with one aspect of physical reality. Together, they constitute your overall experience of life on Earth. As you reduce the aspects of the shape, your energy field is reduced along with your experience or perception. Therefore, expanding your perception in such a way as to experience all 32 dimensional aspects of your being at once—which is the process of blending with your Spirit Self—is the ultimate experience of human multi-sensory perception.

Your electrical nature is subject to physical laws. The ones that are mostly related to your creative powers and mind expansion are the laws of attraction and the law of reflectivity. These laws dictate that the electrical signals you emit will attract similar frequencies and will also reflect the vibrational frequencies of others around you. The more charged your energy field, the more powerful energy you are able to emit, receive and reflect.

This is a crucial concept in your development to realize that you, as energetic beings, are capable of attracting that which matches your electrical frequency. You are also capable of controlling your own energetic field though your mind energy and thoughts. Therefore, controlling what you are emitting to the world will control that which you will attract. Also, deliberately emitting the frequencies you desire will irrevocably attract their potential outcome. That is the process of energy manipulation: the ultimate control of modifying your electrical charge so that it matches perfectly the desired outcome of your experience.

The Masters who walked your Earth awakened to this process as they remembered their original Divine blueprint. They are called Masters for this very reason: they are deliberately capable of controlling and manipulating their own electromagnetic frequency so that they could manifest and experience precisely that which they desire.

They discover the frequency of the Divine Source while being in the flesh, choose to align with that frequency continuously and eventually become that vibration itself. Your Masters are capable of tremendous reflective power as they become the living formula and divine vibrational frequency in the flesh.

You will ask if any human is capable of such energetic awareness and control, and we will assume you have recognized your divine blueprint and nature which allows you access to the divine knowledge of all the Masters. You must realize that the purpose of these Masters IS to teach and lead you to this very fact and recognition so that you ALL may become the Masters you desire. While you each have your own formula and genetic arrangement and chose to journey at your own pace, you have indeed the same full potential of this self-realization and Divine attainment.

MAINTAINING PHYSICAL AND EMOTIONAL HEALTH...

Your physical health is the reflection of your chemical balance while your mental health is mostly related to your electrical balance. However since both aspects are continuously interrelated, you may consider one as an aspect of the other. In general terms, physical balance cannot be accomplished without mental or emotional balance and vice versa. Determining the cause of a chemical imbalance is typically realizing its electrical counterpart. Realizing both facets of the imbalance will drastically reduce its frequency or most likely eradicate its occurrence altogether.

Illness or physical imbalance can be the result of environmental or outer toxicity on the physical body. However, more often than not, it is the result of emotional overload which manifests as a physical imbalance. It is an opportunity to address whatever emotional issue you may be encountering and help you expel its negative effects out of your system. Illness gathers your emotional blocks and negative thoughts into an organ or a tissue and brings them to your attention through physical symptoms so you may relieve yourself from this "negative" burden.

Physical symptoms are your inherent guidance system, a warning sign so to speak that you must attend to a physical as well as emotional predicament occurring in your life. Continuous exposure to such stress will produce more severe symptoms which can still at any time be reversed. With regular and maintained "check and balance" on the physical and emotional level, your chemical and electrical balance is perpetually sustained and debilitating illness is unable to manifest.

Your current medical system typically regards one aspect as the only cause of the imbalance and disregards the other, reason for which most imbalances are chronic, produce relapses or yet transfer to other organs. While your medical sciences offer many satisfactory options for the cure of significant physical malfunctions, you must know that your physical body has an inherent powerful healing mechanism which allows rehabilitation and recovery from any physical or mental imbalance.

Proper diagnostic techniques also play an important part in determining an appropriate treatment for the imbalance or the ailment. Since your cell bodies have an inherent electromagnetic frequency, an imbalance of an organ or system can be measured and corrected at its core by reestablishing the proper frequency of that organ or system. Treatments based on the realignment of meridians lines and vibrational energy at the cellular level with the appropriate chemical support are indeed the perfected way to approach and heal a physical imbalance. However, if not combined with the emotional and mind-al realignments, it will continue resurfacing until all aspects are addressed: the vibrational cellular level and their corresponding chemical components as well as the emotional and mind-al state of the patient.

The use of pharmaceuticals may be regarded as a temporary aid to regain this awareness. However no artificially produced chemical will ultimately restore or replace your inherent and perfect electro-chemical balance. Those who are born with an irreversible handicaps may perfectly attain inner balance and joyfully live a fulfilling life. These individuals contribute to their immediate environment as well as society in general by learning to adjust their differences to a "normal" physical and emotional existence and sharing it with others.

THE MASCULINE AND FEMININE ENERGETIC MAKEUP...

Masculine and Feminine are not intended here as sex distinction. Rather, they represent atomic and elemental compositions of your DNA which translate into attributes women and men possess. This atomic distribution between the 2 sexes enables the collective human matrix a perfect energetic balance. It is created, organized and controlled by the Divine Creators of your species. The steady thriving of your recent same-sex attraction is nothing but an attempt to re-balance the feminine atomic distribution in your human matrix since it had been lacking the past few thousand years. Your collective human genetic makeup is being transmuted to a perfectly balanced and stable state. The apparent imbalances which you observe today are in fact in alignment with the evolutionary codes dictating the proper emancipation of your entire species' attributes and qualities.

6

If You Think Your Thoughts Are Private, Think Again!

This subject and chapter were part of my own self-development and discovery as I began communicating unconsciously with the spirit world. I had to learn and uncover for my self whom or what I was communicating with, and make the distinction between my own thoughts and those originating from an outside source. My invisible friends certainly guided me through the process but it was through my own efforts and discipline that I came to such realization.

This was also a turning point in my life as I suddenly opened my mind to an entire invisible reality which is in fact more real than the one we are all focused in. These experiences and understanding were so powerful that I have dedicated a separate book to them hoping to guide others through the same process.

"Discerning your thoughts does not equal understanding the workings of the Mind. The former is merely a function of the latter" my tutor said.

At times, my invisible teachers would subject me to "severe" teachings in which I would experience a variety of mind communication without knowing the process before hand. I would find myself taken in sudden deep trances unexpectedly and inexplicably. During these trance states, my guides would reflect visions of myself in another life expression or the memory of my pre-natal emergence in physical form. As I awakened from these experiences, they would explain that communication is not only accomplished verbally but through the spontaneous connection to a frequency which equals an entire set of information and experiences. Therefore, all that our mind experiences IS a form of communication with our Spirit Self, other beings as well as other frequencies containing a myriad of information.

◆   ◆   ◆

Consciousness has no physical form. Like energy, it has a vibrational frequency. It is transmitted through thought and then translated through language. While invisible to you, these thought clusters have physical form and represent the "materialized" aspect of consciousness.

Your scientists know the basic techniques in measuring the frequency of thoughts but their main focus has been to use this knowledge for the secretive purpose of mental spying, mind experimentation and control. This knowledge will flourish only when it becomes aligned with the intention of enlightenment, contributing to your spiritual and mind expansion.

YOUR THOUGHTS DO NOT DISAPPEAR...

Consciousness, thoughts and language are different in their physical sense but similar in their elemental sense. One is the materialized aspect of the other.

The World of Thought is a range of frequencies which fall above or below human perceptual field. You may think that thoughts are abstract and can disappear but they are actual energetic clusters which ALWAYS manifest somewhere in space: they either materialize in this layer of reality or one which you may not perceive. They never simply disappear from existence. As with all energy, once created, thoughts can be transmuted but never destroyed.

Your collective thoughts co-exist in one giant web which covers a wide range of wave frequencies. You may have access to all frequencies at any time but you choose to tune in or out of the frequencies your mind is giving attention to. If you accept this mode of communication as a physical fact you can call real, then you will be able to hear your Spirit Self and guidance messages loud and clear. If however, you are not accepting of this form of communication, then your thoughts will be a series of insignificant and incoherent mind chatter and you will automatically dismiss their relevance and value.

You are continuously receiving messages and thoughts from other portions of your own psyche, which you call the sub-conscious, the super-conscious or the Spirit Self. You may also receive information from another consciousness or mind which has aligned with yours for one reason or another. Individuals performing any sort of focused creative work, such as writing or painting for example, typically draw inspiration from their own super-conscious mind or from that of other consciousness aligned with their own. It is at first difficult to discern which thoughts generate from your own elevated psyche and which come from another source. You are able to make that distinction simply by focusing and inquiring about the thought or idea you are receiving. With time, you will be able to acquire such clarity and will naturally familiarize yourself with the workings of your own psyche.

DISCERNING YOUR THOUGHTS...

Discerning and controlling the influx of your thoughts is of utmost importance in realizing what you are emitting to the world in terms of energy and what you are receiving. By law, your thought will attract vibrations of similar frequency and energetic potential. Also, thoughts travel faster than the speed of light and can create powerfully. One thought can lead to instant bliss and another one to degenerative disease.

Spirit and other invisible beings, physical and non-physical, communicate with you all the time, through the exchange of thoughts via radio-like frequency waves. As you begin to familiarize yourself with your thinking mechanism, you will start discerning those thoughts that are coming to you from your Spirit Self, those arising from your subconscious, as well as discern those thoughts originating from an outside source.

Consider the following thought categories:

* Loud thoughts, talking to yourself or mind chatter: These thoughts come from your physical conscious self as you try to process information and resolve problems from your 3-dimensional perspective. These are the thoughts that you must quiet down in order to receive information from your Spirit Self and guidance system.

* Very subtle thoughts which feel like inspiration: These thoughts do not sound like real words, they translate more like a gut feeling or intuition. They typically originate from your Spirit Self. This is your guidance system focused in the Universal Truth which is aware of your spiritual journey and is sending you messages accordingly. Spirit guides may also translate their telepathic communication into inspiration or gut feeling which subtly mixes with your individual thoughts.

* Thoughts, words or sentences which you hear clearly—basically voices. They seem to jump in and interrupt your own thinking process. You know they are not yours because they sound more like statements which you cannot change. You may hear words or a language you are

not familiar with. These may come from spirit guides, other entities or invisible physical beings independent of you. It is important to identify the quality of the information you are receiving and that the accompanying <u>feeling</u> is loving and wise. Otherwise, you have the choice to reject it immediately and focus your mind on a positive thought pattern.

* Other people's thoughts: these voices are quite clear as you can actually hear the other person's mental voice while they are in your presence and therefore know that this message or comment is generated from their psyche and not yours.

In general terms, the above thought categories are all part of your daily experience and must be examined in terms of positive and negative impact on your well-being. Regardless of its origin, if a thought does not feel good, then it is not aligned with the Source of Love and Goodness and is therefore detrimental to your growth and health. On the other hand, thoughts that feel good trigger a sense of well-being and should contribute to effortless materialization of your intent.

The knowledge and discernment of thoughts is intended to accelerate your understanding and grasp of your invisible reality. Moreover, it is aimed for you to take charge of your own minds and creative powers in order to direct your thoughts cautiously, consciously and positively so you may avoid falling victim to deceitful visible or invisible beings or influences.

There is no source of Evil in the Universe. However, there are such things as evil or negative thoughts and energies created by humans and other beings within the human mind matrix. Therefore you may unintentionally become subjected to a transient negative thought or being, physical or non-physical. The Divine laws dictate that no evil energy can be forced upon a human unless it is invited by him, consciously or unconsciously. By becoming aware of the thoughts you are generating, and mastering what you invite into your awareness, you may at any time command ANY influence or thought to stop or vanish and immediately restore your mind and spiritual wellbeing. The laws of your Divine Creator are made of Love energy and are indeed infallible.

PSYCHICS, CHANNELERS AND MEDIUMS...

The world of thought offers access to others' psyche. Psychics and clairvoyants alike tune into your psychic makeup (which includes your memory bank) in order to convey their view of the issue posed. Since they are invited by you, they are easily able to retrieve any information relevant to your question and recognize the experiences linked to a particular event or person. If you are inquiring about a deceased relative, they are able to retrieve from your memory bank your most intimate memories with that individual. It may or may not mean that the deceased person is present at the time of the session. It may appear as so when, in fact, the psychic or medium is telepathically communicating with the deceased relative or simply invoking memories or information from his psyche and relaying them onto you. More often than not, deceased individuals will depart this physical reality within 3 and half days after passing and their shift in consciousness will only allow a faint memory of their life on Earth. Thus they are unable to remember clearly and communicate directly with relatives still in the flesh as they rapidly make their way to other realms of awareness. You may compare this shift in consciousness to your waking from your sleep state when you hardly recognize or remember your experience in your dreams.

Channelers and mediums allow the spirit embodiment of another being who is not in physical form. This is normally agreed upon in a pre-natal arrangement but is seldom recognized as such. The two spirits are typically of the kindred kind and will join in the physical reality at the pre-contracted time. The purpose of such arrangement is for the invited spirit, which is normally a larger body of evolved souls, to access physical reality through the material apparatus of their counterpart. They are able to participate in various experiences with the individual in the flesh as well as convey messages of importance to the physical realm. They will typically utilize the vocal cords of the individual in the flesh and operate within the cognitive restrictions of that individual.

It must also be clarified that spirit may not inhabit another person's body in physical form unless invited by him, knowingly or unknowingly. Therefore, claims of possessions and poltergeists are temporary and harmless infringements of this Divine agreement that can be rectified by the individual recognizing these laws as irrefutable and claiming his/her freedom from the distracting entity.

Psychics and clairvoyants access and retrieve information from the world of probability. They are able to observe and confirm future events only when the momentum of your intentions and thoughts is strong enough that the outcome may not be stopped. More often than not, you are still able to change the outcome if you choose to. You are always in charge of your destiny and the psychic's insight should be used solely as guidance. Psychics who attempt to predict world events tap into a global consciousness which is more convoluted and continuously being rearranged. As one person thinks, he/she triggers a shift in the frequency of the collective matrix which then determines a new outcome. The only true prophecies are those revealed from the divine realms at very rare and auspicious times when they usher your collective destiny into its next evolutionary stage.

While there is much controversy surrounding this subject, the benefit that psychics, channelers and mediums have introduced to your awareness is the enhancement of your belief and gradual understanding of the existence of the invisible spirit world. In that sense, they have contributed to your exploration of the unseen worlds. However, true spiritual expansion is of a personal nature between your consciousness and that of your Divine Creator.

THE WORLD OF PROBABILITY...

Without potential or probability, there would be no experience. If you always know the outcome of every thought or action, you would not be able to experience it. Your experience in the physical will be futile indeed.

Each time you think, you release information about your desires to the Universe, which translates it into a form of energy that can either materialize or create a new reality in another dimensional layer or field. However, you can be certain that ALL you are thinking IS materializing or being transmuted in one form of energy or another.

For this reason, the world of thought is also the realm of eventuality or probability. Your thoughts manifest and carry their own intent in this or another reality. Similarly, negative thoughts which do not materialize here will remain energetically attached to your consciousness. Relinquishing all negative thoughts, even those which do not materialize in this reality, will facilitate and expedite your spiritual healing and purification. For thoughts are energetic clusters that once produced may be transmuted but never destroyed.

The purpose of the realm of probability is to allow you to re-examine your choice or intent within the time/space continuum and evaluate their significance upon your spiritual expansion. In retrospect, you will realize that all the thoughts which have materialized in your physical reality carried an intent which was necessary to your spiritual evolution, whereas those that did not were not as crucial precursors to your awakening. This does not imply that a fatalistic attitude should be adopted regarding your thinking process. Rather, it is to carefully examine your thoughts as they are launched into the Universe, acknowledge yourself as a powerful co-creator with the Cosmic Forces, and trust their perpetual precise and perfect work regarding your awakening.

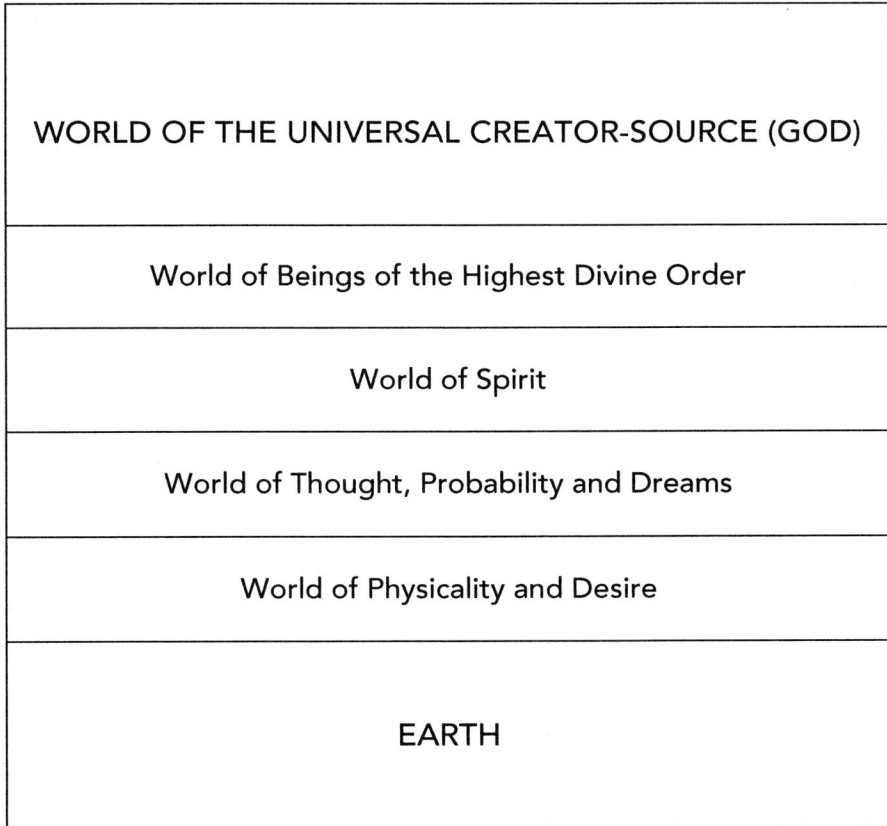

WORLD OF THE UNIVERSAL CREATOR-SOURCE (GOD)
World of Beings of the Highest Divine Order
World of Spirit
World of Thought, Probability and Dreams
World of Physicality and Desire
EARTH

FIGURE 7: Hierarchy of the Visible and Invisible Worlds

THE WORLD OF DREAMS...

The world of dreams is part of the world of probability as it is the continuation, so to speak, of those thoughts which have not materialized in your physical life. It corresponds to a set of brain wave frequencies which allow the exploration of various states of consciousness and realities. The governing factors which define this world are non-physical, therefore they do not encounter the same laws and limitations of your awakened states.

The world of dreams uses a language which is highly symbolic and subjective. The images created in your dream state represent meanings which are subject to your individual interpretation of reality. For example, dreaming of the ocean may represent freedom, mind expansion or sexual release for some, whereas for others, it may represent their fear of dying etc...

The dream language is highly symbolic and conceptual, not literal, which means that the overall meaning of the dream symbolizes a *particular emotion* or experience and its literal translation does not apply. For example, if you dream that you are swimming in the ocean and drowned, this does not imply that you should not go into the ocean because it is dangerous and you may drown. It may simply mean that you may be fearful of a particular life experience coming up in your physical life etc. This is one simplistic explanation since dreams are subject to the individual's interpretation of their own experience.

Dreams have several purposes and may be used in a variety of ways. We will attempt to identify the various ways dreams can be experienced so you may fully benefit from their existence and use.

The purpose of dreams can be summarized and simplified as follows:

1. Dreams allow you to resolve unfinished thoughts. The thousands of thoughts that you generate each day which do not manifest in your physical reality continue existing in one parallel reality called the world of dreams. If you have been thinking of a new opportunity and your physical reality has not materialized it yet, these thoughts will manifest in your dream state as unfinished. You will continue dreaming about the possibility of this opportunity and will be able to experience what it will feel like to have it before it actually materializes. The world of dreams and probability gives you alternative options and emotions regarding this particular event.

2. The dream world is an opportunity to make a conscious choice of what you wish to manifest in your awakened reality. The *emotions* associated with your dream are your guidance system in making that choice. If the emotions you experience in your dream state are positive, then you will likely attract a positive outcome regarding your choice. It is imperative to pay attention to the emotions associated with the dream rather than its content alone so you may take appropriate steps accordingly.

3. The dream world is the medium through which you channel the negative emotions and the fears you experience during your awakened state. When you have minimal negative thoughts, emotions or fears during your awakened state, these are normally neutralized and absorbed by the positive and loving thoughts you simultaneously generate. However, if the amount of negative thoughts exceeds that of the positive ones, their residue may appear in your dream state in the form of disturbing, recurring dreams or nightmares. The world of dreams is the cleansing ground for your fears and is a way to channel your negativity out of your physical reality. You may therefore regard the negative emotions associated with nightmares as a result of a negative overflow, so to speak, of your awakened reality.

4. The world of dreams allows you to explore other realities, parallel worlds and connect with other beings other than through the physical medium. During your awakened state, you may have inquired about another being and your relationship with them. Your dreams will respond to your request by offering an encounter with those beings in question. These experiences are non-physical but entirely real.

5. The world of dreams is the frequency where you Spirit Self resides. It is there that it connects with your physical self as well as other aspects of your self so you may explore your non-physicality. It should be noted that all such experiences are real even if they do not translate in your physical life.

6. The world of dreams is also the medium in which you access and activate your cellular memory and that which is imprinted in your

memory bank. Through your dreams, you are able to recall your pre-natal agreement and be guided again on the proper path which you have selected prior to incarnating physically. While you are normally unable to recall these dreams, they still remain in your subconscious mind during your awakened state and will continue guiding you on your pre-arranged path.

7. Your Spirit Self as well as your spirit guides who normally guide you during your awakened state through emotions, thoughts or inspiration, use the dream world for guidance or warning of distractions and negative impact on your physical wellbeing. You may consider certain dreams as a premonition of an event. However, it is always a conscious choice to bring that dream about into your physical reality. If the momentum for that event is too strong to prevent it from manifesting, then this dream may be considered as a premonition and will then help you prepare to deal with its consequences.

8. The world of dreams answers your questions. As you think, you materialize some thoughts and let go of others. These thoughts continue on in the world of dreams and offer you answers depicted in your dreams. They can be as mundane as a meal recipe or as crucial to your spiritual growth as your pre-natal agreement. The world of dreams is purposeful rather than a set of random and insignificant imagery or messages.

As you begin to acknowledge the vast levels of realities your consciousness is able to explore, your will become a proficient and conscious creator of your experience. You will begin a cognizant telepathic communication with your Spirit Self and will cease to succumb to the fears of your nightmares. You will also embrace these magnificent cleansing and healing systems encoded in your being and will become grateful for their powerful contribution to your spiritual enrichment. The worlds of thought, dreams and probability are undeniably invisible. However they are more real than your physical self as they function under the Universal Laws of your Divine Creator which are indeed eternal and absolute.

7

Divine and Human Creation

As I mentioned in the introduction of this book, I seemed to be aware of the human creative process since I was a young child. I wonder if that is the case for all children and they simply chose to ignore their gift or that their environment is simply not conducive to such understanding and experimentation. I personally learned to survive my childhood by becoming an obstinate observer and relentless inquisitor regarding all that I witnessed and experienced.

I was guided to discover the Universal Laws affecting the human creative process through books and teachings but these experiences were mere reminders of what I had always known. In an instant, all made perfect sense and thanks to my divine teachers, all fell apart as well: as I began to consciously apply these laws, I also began to encounter their opposite effect. This awareness brought me to the next realization that the laws applicable to the creative process function within the realm of duality, hence the distinction between human and divine creation. I wanted to create with the tools of divinity and transcend this world of duality. "Indeed, it is possible", they said, "Only if you were God...And all humans ARE indeed God, therefore it is possible." Wow, this is powerful...

◆   ◆   ◆

THOUGHT is the tool for all Creative Consciousness, Human or Divine. At the Source, Creation occurs through the FIRST THOUGHT and the subsequent creative process is established henceforth. The Creator-Mind creates and controls matter through Thought. And since the Creator-Mind energy is innate in all beings, Thought is the tool by which all intelligent beings create and procreate.

CREATION is the conceptualization and bringing about of new energy in one form or another. An idea, a relationship or a house are different forms of the same process. They are brought about by the Mind-Energy (your thoughts) and manifest in abstract or physical forms. The elemental form of each creation is what determines the shape it manifests in.

Your continuous decision-making is also creation. As you make a choice regarding your actions, thoughts, relationships, desires etc., you are indeed creating your own reality.

The human creative process works in conjunction with cosmic forces and agencies. When the human Mind-Energy is activated, the proper cosmic forces collapse the atomic composition of the idea and transmute its elements appropriately so that it may manifest physically. However, humans instinctively create in duality, positive and negative, with masculine and feminine focus, while Divine Beings only create with pure Light and Sound energies.

THE DIVINE CREATIVE FORMULA...

INFINITY is Pure Consciousness which *personalizes* in the Creator-Source. You may say that the Creator-Source is the First Uncaused Reality, Being and Consciousness of Infinity. Or that the Creator-Source is the self-created and focused *thought* of Infinity.

The Creator-Source's attributes inherent within its own Being are pure Love, Truth and Beauty. It is also the Universal Mind-Energy which created (through the First Thought) its own expression and manifestation (the Universal Body-Energy) as well as its own nature and functioning (the Universal Spirit-Energy).

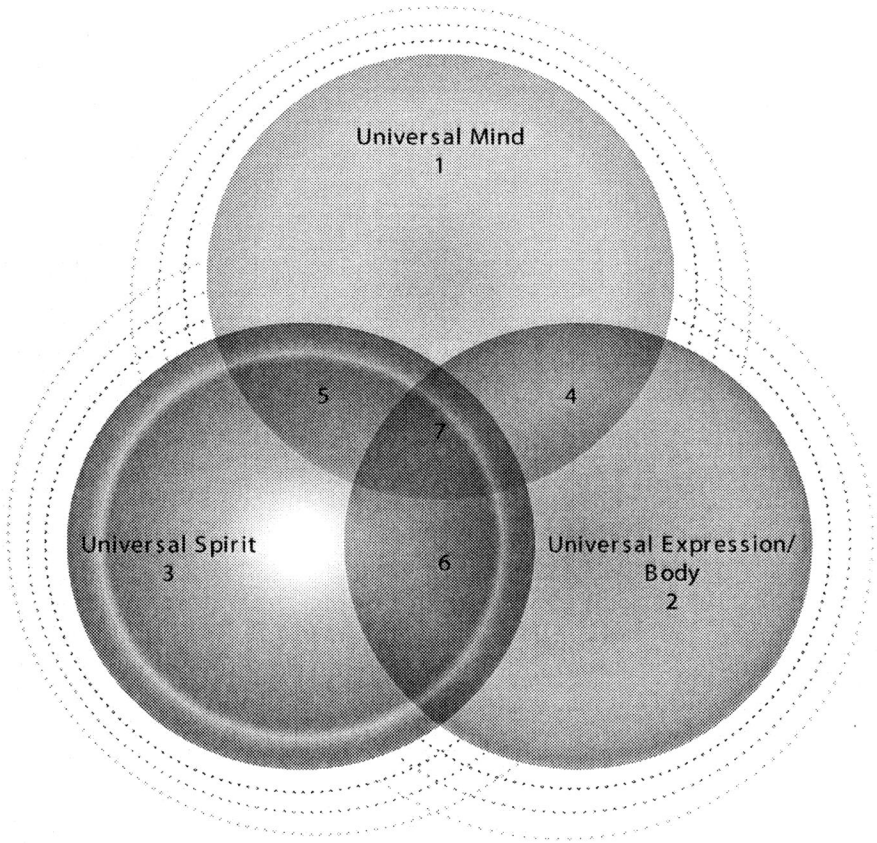

FIGURE 8: The Creator-Source.

There are therefore 7 aspects of the Creator-Source. Once created, these 7 aspects become Beings and Consciousness with their own characteristics, while sharing at once the characteristics of the Creator-Source. All subsequent creations are the result of deliberate action and thought in one of the combinations of these 7 aspects of the Creator-Source:

1. Universal Mind-Energy

2. Universal Mind-Energy + Universal Expression/Body Energy

3. Universal Mind-Energy + Universal Spirit Energy

4. Universal Mind-Energy + Universal Expression/Body Energy + Universal Spirit Energy

5. Universal Expression/Body Energy

6. Universal Expression/Body-Energy + Universal Spirit Energy

7. Universal Spirit Energy

Together, all 7 aspects of the Creator-Source, manifest and function throughout their created worlds through the Cosmic Mind. Subsequently, Divine Creation is based on a 7-denomination principle, each representing one aspect of the 7 aspects of the Creator-Source. Each creation may also have patterns of 3, 10 or 12 denominations depending on its expression and purpose.

Divine Creators create physical realities through light and sound bending and manipulation. When Light and Sound are bent, they appear in another reality with new sets of conditions and rules. Your world is created in such a way as to absorb a minute portion of the cosmic energy emanating from your Divine Creator's abode in the center of your Major Universe. The colors, light and sound vibrations which exist in your system are the product of manipulation and bending of the same energies at their source.

The Divine formula, from pure energy to materialization, can be simplified as follows:

DIVINE CREATION is <u>Divine Thought</u> = Divine Sound/Light = Divine Frequency = Divine Mathematical Formula = Divine Atomic Element = <u>Divine Manifestation</u>. The Divine thought is therefore Divine manifestation and it is spontaneous: which means that the Divine thought-intent is automatic creation. The attributes inherent in the Creator-Source are pure Love, Truth and Beauty and therefore Divine Creation can only manifest with such attributes.

At the Creator-Source, consciousness is likened to pure positive energy. It is absolute and "perfect", indeed. However, each time the Creator-Source creates, a particle of its energy splits off and becomes its own being or consciousness. This created consciousness carries a minute portion of the memory of its Creator and it remains eternally connected to Him through an energetic "umbilical cord".

Universes upon universes are thus created and with each creation, the particles of the Universal Mind, Body or Spirit split off into more minute and more finite consciousness. The more finite a creation is, the more "imperfect" it becomes due to its remoteness from the original Creator-Source. Evolutionary worlds, such as yours, occupy a string of energy farthest from the Source and thus your species' infinitesimal consciousness requires millennia of mind expansion in order to perfectly grasp the meaning of the Creator-Source and the mysteries of Creation.

As such, while you carry the blueprint of your Divine Creator within the essence of your being, your energetic formula (which is finite or "imperfect") cannot sustain a direct encounter or blending with Him who is infinite. Your atomic composition will simply rupture and disintegrate unless you evolve to an energetic frequency high enough to withstand His massive Light and energetic power. Therefore, the expansion of your soul is the method by which you, as evolutionary material beings, gradually transmute into a more perfected and expanded atomic formula which can blend with your Divine Creator.

THE HUMAN CREATIVE FORMULA...

You exist in a remote physical place in the Universe where awareness is finite and most limited. You function in a realm of emotions, beliefs and incomprehensible laws. Not unlike your Divine Creators, you create through Thought. However, your thoughts are subject to your physicality and will materialize according to the following formula:

HUMAN CREATION = Thought + Desire + Belief + Surrender

THOUGHT is the asking, the conscious choice and focus of your intent.

DESIRE is the impetus, the fuel or passion of your intent.

> BELIEF is the knowledge of self and faith in your potential.
>
> SURRENDER is your recognition as a Co-creator with the Divine order and your oneness with the Universal Forces which assist you in the materialization of your intent.

Thought, without desire, belief or surrender will not materialize. Desire without focused intent, belief or surrender will not materialize. Most of all, thought, desire and belief without surrender will not materialize for as you think, you must be assisted by cosmic forces and elementals who convert your thoughts into things. You are co-creators of reality. You cannot exist and create outside the Creator-Mind or without the divine beings and forces of the Universe.

The way these cosmic forces and elementals work depends on the type of information they are given. If your thought is aligned with a universal cause, they will trigger a large amount of energy which involves a large potential—which, in turn, will have a larger impact. However, if your thought is about material possession, they will employ the frequency of the physical reality by provoking the appropriate circumstances and guide you towards your goal.

If your thought manifested immediately and spontaneously, the perfect conditions may not have an opportunity to germinate properly. Evolved beings that are more familiar with the workings of the mind and their creative powers are able to manifest spontaneously as they think. Yet only when you have reached that level of spiritual maturity and have mastered this formula, will you then have no need to incarnate in the physical, and will advance to more elaborate ways of creating in the higher realms. Your human life will then be complete.

POSITIVE AND NEGATIVE CREATION...

When you think, your positive emotions create a vibrational pattern which enhance your energetic field and create positively, while your negative emotions create negatively and ultimately shut down your electromagnetic operational system. Your creative formula does not discern positive from negative thoughts. It is there to manifest them. YOU are in charge of this discernment and being in control of the type of frequency you want to emit and receive.

Negative thoughts are self-destructive because they neither derive from nor thrive on the energy of the Creator-Source. Continuous and large amounts of negative thoughts lead to isolation from the whole and eventually disintegration. There is a way to survive in the pool of human negative energy by continuously aligning with your Divine Creator who is pure Love energy. Thoughts travel faster than the speed of light and have no obstacles. You can reverse your negative thoughts and transmute them instantly into the positive frequency of Love.

THE LAWS OF ATTRACTION AND REFLECTIVITY...

Energy's vibrational nature dictates that it will attract all that which is similar to its frequency and will repel that which is not. If you emit an emotion or thought which is positively charged, it will attract other emotions or thoughts charged similarly. If observed carefully, your outer experience is but the reflection of your inner thinking mechanism. When you ask for a successful career but attract failure or disappointment, study carefully the subconscious thoughts and emotions which may have triggered those circumstances. Your subconscious self dictates the outcome of your experience. More often than not, your subconscious is based negatively while you think you are creating positively.

Negative circumstances are not always the result of negative thoughts. Through your physical experience, which is a realm of duality, you will indubitably attract negative or uncomfortable situations even when you are conscious of your positive thought patterns. These apparently negative circumstances are but the verification of your faith and surface when it is necessary for you to strongly discern what you want or do not want in your life experience. In other words, they are opportunities for you, who are always in charge, to make a choice. Some negative experiences appear so powerfully that they engender more of the same and will contribute to your further confusion and disconcertment. However, as you evolve, you begin to recognize these situations as an opportunity for consciousness expansion and immediately transmute them into positive ones within a relatively short time.

Another important law of the human creative mechanism is the Law of Reflectivity which dictates that your electromagnetic nature is mirrored in other individuals and circumstances. The purpose of your Earthly experience is to enhance your mind expansion by mastering your creative skills. Reflectivity is yet another main tool you may utilize to see the reflection of your own intent, thoughts and emotions projected onto others.

Your social nature stems from your inner reflective nature to see yourselves into others so you may comprehend more of the characteristics of your own being. When you ask to know who you are, you will attract individuals and circumstances reflecting back to you parts of your own self. Only when you begin to recognize these traits, do you become able to heal or master them. Exceptionally powerful beings transmit a tremendous amount of electrical charge so that their reflectivity may be overwhelming. The great Masters and healers of your time can be at once tremendously loved and tremendously feared as individuals who come in contact with them either see the potential of their loving nature or the reflection of their exemplified fears.

Reflectivity is also the process by which you know who you are according to those who perceive you. It is an exercise of faith in your own self which allows you to discern your inner truths from those that others impose upon you. From an outer perspective, you are defined according to how you are perceived by others and therefore you may have as many interpretations of who you are as there are individuals observing you. Your task is to remain focused on your inner truth, as the tool of reflectivity is powerful indeed.

The law of reflectivity also implies your "everywhereness". Everywhere you look is a reflection of who you are. The only physical and tangible evidence in your world is the mirror. If you stand before a mirror and look at yourself, you will realize that there are now two of you in 2 spaces at the same time. If your eyes meet another individual at one particular point in space, you are now reflecting another type of your "everywhereness". You are reflecting yourself through all beings and things through an invisible energetic matter and not only thought: because your Spirit Self is your vibrational match but it is not limited by time or space, then it is indeed capable of perceiving through all physical obstacles, behind you, below you, beside you and above you. "Everywherness" is a condition of the state you are in: in the physical that is. Together with your Spirit Self, you and all physical beings form an entire universe of entities collaborating and reflecting each other's vibrational energy at any given time.

COSMIC REFLECTIVITY...

Divinity is also based on reflectivity as a method of purification, healing or expansion. While the process may appear disagreeable from a human perspective, it should be embraced and used to your advantage and evolution process once you realize its true and divine purpose. This physical and illusionary paradigm is the practice ground of the law of reflectivity. As you begin to recognize portions of yourself enhanced, magnified and refracted by the mirror that others provide you, your experience and energetic exchange with others will serve to heal, transmute and purify your soul and mind so you may progress to the higher realms of creation.

Cosmic balance is similarly achieved through the law of reflectivity. Planetary systems, created stars and suns reflect their individual energetic pattern onto their neighboring organisms. You will notice than Mars, for example, reflects your planet's patterns and physical formations. As you observe structural "similarities" on Mars, these similarities are in fact the reflection of your own planetary physical arrangement. While your scientists believe they are observing Mars only as a planet of the past and may thereby predict Earth's future, they are in fact merely analyzing the projection of your current Earth's physical characteristics onto the planet Mars. In other words, the physical observations and discoveries on Mars detect what your current Earth's frequency allows. If Earth was shifted into a new cosmic location and hence vibration, you would automatically observe different life patterns and characteristics on the same planet Mars.

Furthermore, your physical apparatus—your body—and scientific instruments provide a limited understanding of this much larger and multi-layered reality of other planets. Your Earth's reflectivity onto your neighboring planet thus helps you identify your own structural status but does not necessarily offer a truthful or complete study of the examined planet.

ABOUT CLONING...

There is much controversy in your world about the reproduction of human life within laboratory confines and through scientific means for therapeutic or simply gene cloning purposes. The key resides in the fact that reproducing human cells does not imply creating life. Human life consists of the vital aspects of your physical body—that which you are reproducing—and a consciousness or soul that which can only be formulated by the evolved Consciousness of your Divine Creator. While certain gene characteristics and combinations may predispose individuals to certain behaviors, the reproduction of a *consciousness* may never be achieved through your scientific experimentation and laboratories as implied in your debates.

8

The Purpose of Earthly Life

I am certainly not the first to ask "who are we?" and "what are we doing her?" I decided to include this section in my book when, during one of my moments of despair, my beloved spirit teacher serenely announced that my only purpose in this Earthly expression was "consciousness expansion". What? Is that it?! That was certainly of no help at all!...Until I began to truly experience what was meant by this powerful revelation...

Since that disappointing announcement, my spirit teachers tenaciously followed my daily routine, pointing out every thought, every action, every conversation, every meal and every intent as a unique physical experience contributing to my consciousness expansion. There is not one instant in a day that does not fulfill such a grand purpose and it is orchestrated perfectly by the Spirit Self, which is cognizant of this dimension and all other realities at once. "It is a perfect journey leading to one eventual and glorious destination", they said, "the ultimate blending with the Creator-Father and the Creator-Source". They continued: "Without the constant expansion of your consciousness, you are unable to sustain His tremendous power and energy proliferation". I have since become a truthful and studious selector of every moment of my day, knowing that it is taking me a step closer or step away from the Divine Mind and Spirit of my Creator. Thank you my beautiful friends in Heaven!

◆   ◆   ◆

Creation is a focused and precise energetic process. It is intentional and purposeful. Divine Beings create with the purpose of perpetuity and their creations henceforth have eternal potential. Once a creation is accomplished, it becomes its own being and consciousness and will create its own purpose within the laws that created it.

DEFINING EVOLUTION...

The physical worlds (planets, stars, galaxies, and more) do commence in a time and space context and have an evolutionary pattern. However, once they reach a ripe state which can serve their purpose, they will adjust intermittently to maintain and eventually stabilize within their intended patterns. Your Earth, for example, evolved physically over several billion years to a point of developing an atmosphere capable of sustaining human life. It is now inhabited by you and will intermittently adjust its pulse and frequency, through floods, earthquakes and volcano eruptions, to maintain its chemical and electromagnetic balance within the galactic arrangement.

The evolution of a created species such as humans, on the other hand, does not exist in the linear sense. It does exist as *Consciousness Expansion*. Therefore, a reality in which consciousness can be expanded through creative experimentation is implemented for all evolutionary physical beings. When you use the physical realms as your practice ground to create your reality, you are expanding your consciousness and therefore getting one step closer to the Divine techniques of Creation and higher realms of existence.

THE COLLECTIVE AGREEMENT...

The collective human agreement is the process by which each individual is contributing energetically to the balancing of the planet en masse. As the planet evolves its consciousness, you as a group are assisting her process and allowing her consciousness expansion. Your individual thoughts and creativity play a part in the overall Earthly creative plan, as you are naturally providing that which she needs in terms of energy manifestation. The mineral and animal kingdoms are also harmonizing your Earth's chemical and electrical pulses and breathing patterns.

You come into this reality knowing about the physical laws, otherwise you could not materialize. However, you choose this medium to learn and understand the greater Universal Laws which govern Creation. Here you discover the essence of your own being as well as the principles of the Universal Laws simultaneously, as part of discovering yourself *is* the discovery of the Universal Laws which govern your planet.

Self-discovery happens not only through self-reflection but also through the work you do with others and for others. If you choose life's circumstances carefully, you will encounter situations that allow you to experience portions of yourself you are NOT familiar with: those characteristics which are still unknown to you. It is a necessary arrangement, a game plan which you have co-created with your Divine Creators.

While you may find it difficult to believe from your current perspective that you, as in all humans, may have co-created such a trying game as your Earthly existence, you may consider some of the creations you are responsible for in your current physical life: You create mind games and weapons and simultaneously grieve for the victims of your quarrels and wars. You accept self-destruction through substance or physical abuse and concurrently complain of your own ill-fate. Even the physically or mentally challenged, or the accidents of time you may succumb to, are consciously or unconsciously self-created conditions. You are indeed the co-creators of your own destiny and reality, collectively as a species.

THE INDIVIDUAL AGREEMENT...

Individually, you are here for one purpose only and that is to expand your consciousness. By learning how to create in a virtual paradigm, you can evolve to more complex ways of creation patterns. This is the ascension process for all humans, from material and evolutionary to purely spiritual. Ascension is not realized upwards. Rather it is a mind and spirit gravitational expansion which draws you inwards, towards the nucleus of your Universe where your Divine Creator resides. This gravitational pull towards the Divine realm is what allows the final merging with the Creator-Source.

In order to recall your current soul agreement, you may very well create it at any time. All agreements are such that they are the direct manifestation of who you are now or, at the very least, choose to be. Whatever you agree to now, IS. If you are unable to conceive it, then it cannot be your agreement and that is law.

AGREEMENTS OF STAR AND CELESTIAL BEINGS...

Those who are of non-human origin and have chosen to incarnate in human form, are also here for a specific purpose. This category includes beings from other more evolved star systems as well as beings of different celestial orders, teachers, guardians…With the exception of very rare cases, these beings will enter this system and incarnate as a human infant. It is the awakening to their original blue-print or state of origin that allows them to remember the purpose and agreement of their particular incarnation. Also, there is an energetic collapse that occurs when they originate in an evolved system and think themselves in a material system such as Earth and the Milky Way. The memory cells and consciousness of these beings cannot normally sustain such a collapse and they will therefore begin life as a normal human infant and awaken gradually to their pre-natal contract. Evolved beings that choose this incarnation are here in service of their Divine Creator and therefore play an important part in ushering humans to a new and enlightened age.

AGREEMENT OF THE DIVINE CREATORS…

Divine Creators, such as the Melchizedeks or those you may call "Sons of God", can appear complete in your planetary system. However, they may also choose to go through the normal awakening process which all humans must go through to experience a true human experi-ence, as they very well know that *experience* indeed is the divine order and not knowledge alone. This materialization is the process by which a Divine Creator can experience the true life of his own crea-tures and assist in their awakening and expansion.

These Divine Beings may become fully aware of their pre-natal arrangement while in the flesh and may choose to remain on the Earthly plane for several hundred years at a time. Their true agreement is indescribable in human terms because it is an agreement with the Creator-Source whose expression has no finite translation. In simpler terms, these divine souls are involved in a plan related to planetary and stellar alignments or other cosmic resonance and spiritual endeav-ors. They are the genetic creators, designers, physical architects and spiritual teachers who are able to adjust physical and non-physical energies so that all beings and things remain in harmony with the Divine whole and the Creator-Source. These divine souls guide and direct humanity into its next phase of existence. Through their tremen-dous power, the Divine Breath of the Creator-Source is carried through and keeps the planet's balance and movement in perfect harmony and alignment with its sister planets and galaxies which fall under their reign and responsibility.

The Divine Creators work in unison with other star and celestial beings while incarnate in human form. They agree to a common plan which is infallible. Their energetic rhythm and resonance perform a flawless and simultaneous uplifting of human and planetary energies. Because of their nature and lineage, they maintain an unbroken communion with the Creator-Source and their divine counterparts in the Higher Realms. Due to its sacred and mostly incomprehensible nature, this communion becomes concealed from human consciousness. It is this sacred communion that makes these Divine Creators the "bridge" to the higher realms and to the Creator-Source. Similarly, it is through this communion that they are able to bring the energy of the Creator-Source (Heaven) into the physical realm and matrix (Earth).

These magnificent beings carry a thousand-fold energetic frequency that of any human and are able to participate in many planetary, even galactic endeavors, at once. They enter your physical realms and de-particularize into a thousand individual beings and entities at times as to spread their energetic fields throughout the worlds they are occupying. They embody the Creator-Source formula itself, which is in fact of their own design. They can also escape physical death through the same creative formula they use to enter. They transcend this realm simply by suspending their powers into the next reality and thinking themselves into manifesting elsewhere. That is the ultimate creative power of all beings: transmuting their own existence from one reality to the next.

9

About Religion...

My inner knowing that most current religious teachings are erroneous, misleading or distorted led me to shun religious congregations and institutions at a very young age. As I grew up, I concluded that these rituals and traditions are unnecessary and hopeless because they do not contribute to human enlightenment or any particularly superior behavior. It seems that we suddenly become generous and loving on some religious occasions, but very few of these feelings are carried through our daily life to achieve universal peace or harmony. Therefore, current religions are not the way leading us to the Love, Truth, Beauty or Goodness which characterize the true nature of a loving "God".

The part on revelation came abruptly and swiftly through dictation, basically. I awoke one morning pressured by my spirit teacher to iterate these concepts and include them in this book, and so I did. The intention is not to criticize, refute or ridicule current religious concepts. Rather, it is simply to remind and guide those seekers of Divine Truth to carry on their journey of self-realization without the guilt or pressure of belonging to an organized school of thought, as so commonly observed in today's society. I am grateful that my Divine Teachers appeared in my life at a young age and taught me that true religion is nothing but my personal experience with the Creator-Father. I am thankful that I became aware of the invisible truths directly and independently of outside influences and so I can now become an example of this magnificent possibility.

◆   ◆   ◆

Religion is defined as "a belief in and worship of God" and "a system of beliefs involving a code of ethics". It is a principle of human understanding of an infinite reality or a limited human perspective of a limitless Creator. The combination of both principles, the finite and the infinite, must merge in a matrix of understanding which is then called Religion.

ABOUT REVELATIONS...

Due to its limitless nature, the transmission of Godly matters cannot fit in a finite, linear and simplistic set of scientific proofs. It must be revealed. Revelation is the process by which Spirit Beings or "God" interact and communicate with a physical being in human form. From Enoch, Abraham and Moses to Buddha and Mohammed, revelations about God and His principles have been transmitted through thought exchange or telepathy, visions and apparitions. The validity and accuracy of such exchange depend on the interpretation of the recipient. Highly evolved Spirit Beings or "God" will not transmit messages to physical beings unable to comprehend or assimilate their meanings. Therefore, these chosen individuals who acknowledge being transmitted information from "God" have themselves evolved enough, on a consciousness level, to accept this mode of communication as a valid mental transmission. These individuals are also lucid enough regarding their individual agreement of their Earthly lives, which consists of receiving such information and translating it to their contemporaries and future fellow humans.

Regardless of the information being transmitted, these enlightened men and women do indeed receive and document information about "God" and His principles. The predicament becomes when these pure thought exchanges are filtered through their respective minds, then translated through human language, which allows only a portion of the pure thought to be expressed. This process becomes further convoluted when these translated messages are then taught to others and additionally translated in other languages. The amount of distortions which occur between the original thought of "God" and the final generations and translations from mind to mind and from language to language are indeed vast.

The Godly messages received by the enlightened individual, while purely understood, are then carried out into your physical world grossly distorted, exaggerated, censored or suppressed depending on the individual and the collective needs and fears of your time. The political, economic and cultural premise of your society will also determine what you are capable of accepting or rejecting in terms of revealed truths or spiritual teachings. If these teachings conflict with your materialistic goals, they will then be concealed and censored to insure "stability" within your societal system.

It is therefore erroneous to think that your current religions are based solely on a pure thought exchange with "God". It is certainly what true religion is intended to be. However, none of your current religions have been fully respectful of the true and original thoughts of the Divine Creator transmitted to his Earthly children of time and space.

The nature of "God" is pure Love, Truth and Beauty. It is unable to discriminate between its creatures. It is revealed purely to all humans in one same language of unification.

The language used by the Celestial Beings transmitting Divine messages to the physical worlds is also highly symbolic: due to the evolutionary nature of your consciousness, you will be told truths in a language which you can comprehend. A few thousand years ago when the Earth was thought to be flat for example, it would have been impossible for the individual to accept and comprehend the concept of a multi-dimensional evolving universe and a Universal Mind or a human mind matrix. Parables are then used to appeal to a wide group of individuals who are thus able to perceive the truth behind the stories being told according to their own spiritual and mind development.

The codes of ethics associated with the different religions are usually related to social or health concerns at the time these revelations occur. The undiscriminating and pure Thought of "God" will not teach one human to fast and be polygamous, while another be baptized and monogamous in order to attain salvation. ALL of the Divine Creator's creatures are endowed *equally* with a particle of the *same* Creator Energy within your individual genetic makeup and memory cells. It is your perception and *interpretation* of the Divine revelations which urge you to congregate under separate and contradictory schools and institutions.

RELIGIOUS TRUTHS AND DISTORTIONS...

We will attempt to reveal the true meaning and distortions of some of the laws and concepts which your current main religions are based on.

SIN: No created being is born a sinner. Humans are able however to create sin deliberately by rejecting the positive energy of love and embracing the destructive energy of evil. It is free will indeed.

ONLY BELIEVERS RECEIVE SALVATION: All humans receive salvation at the time of physical death regardless of their actions in the flesh. However, those who have embraced evil are unable to continue their spiritual journey and consciousness expansion due to the lower energetic frequencies they have accumulated. They must purge and transmute their sins or negative frequencies into a higher and more pure vibration in order to proceed to higher realms of existence.

ETERNAL LIFE: All creatures are created eternal. Those who reject eternity and the Love of the Creator-Source, may also reject the continuation of their own journey. Eternal life is never denied by a discriminating or judgmental Creator.

BAPTISM: Purification of the soul does not occur solely through the act of baptism. Purification of spirit occurs through the intent of the individual seeking his Divine Creator. The act of baptism is symbolic of the intent of the individual. It does not guarantee salvation per se. Your faith and intent do.

MIRACLES: The miracles performed by a human divine being such as Jesus, for example, are real. However, it is the combination of His thought which is the pure conduit of the Creator-Source and the conscious or unconscious faith and total surrender of the individual requesting the miracle which allows the miracle to occur. It is co-creation at its best: Man asking and the Creator giving in a perfect and dynamic energetic exchange.

MONOGAMY OR POLYGAMY: Your human nature allows you to explore and express love through your physical senses in a unique way. Human love is in alignment with the Divine Creator's Love, through sexuality or marriage. If your intent is pure, then you may carry out your love expressions in full respect of the other individuals involved. You can therefore give and receive love within any arrangement while maintaining harmony and truthfulness with the intent and desire of the other.

FASTING: Spiritual expansion is not dependent on your physical diet. It is however based on your body, mind and spirit balance and the respect of creation in general. Your intent of spiritual purification and advancement will naturally lead you individually to a harmonious diet or abstinence of certain foods, without the harmful effects of forced fasting.

KARMIC DEBTS: Karma is the energetic release of your intent and the attraction of its match. If you intend harm to another individual, you release negative and destructive thoughts to the universe which will respond perfectly to your vibration by replicating a negative result. Karma is not a law of punishment. Rather, it is a universal law of energetic attraction. You are in charge of your destiny, indeed.

REINCARNATION: You may appear in one or several thousand lives in human or other physical forms while you carefully and individually select your respective soul and mind journey. You are always however the one same soul, projecting your consciousness in one or more physical bodies, having one or more physical experiences intermittently or at once.

FINDING TRUE RELIGION...

Religion is the process by which the Creator-Source is revealed to you as you are attempting to find Him. You are an extension of the Universal Mind-Body-Spirit of the Creator-Source and you do possess a personal and individual relationship with that Creator-Source through the person of your Divine Creator. True religion is the direct link, the individual and unique relationship between you and your Divine Creator. It is therefore *personal.*

Your social and interactive nature is conducive to sharing experiences with others, including religious ones. Therefore, congregations which offer a powerful merging of positive energies can be supportive and helpful in your quest for Divine Truth. However, those groupings and institutions which are based on punishment or fear or those who claim to be the only possible way to attain salvation are not the reflection of the wisdom or truth of your Divine Creator.

LIVING THE PERFECTED RELIGIOUS LIFE...

Religion is your personal experience with your Divine Creator. While it may be shared or enhanced by others, it is only through your own individual and personal experience that true religion can be practiced.

True religion is also your guide for mind expansion as well as spiritual realization. It manifests through all aspects of your physical life, including your work, your physical body, your social circle and most of all your true beliefs and thoughts. In order to live the perfect religious life while in the flesh, you may consider the following:

- Your THOUGHTS and intentions must be directed positively, in alignment with your mental and spiritual expansion and the Spirit of your Divine Creator.

- Your ACTIONS must be aligned with the Love energy of your Divine Creator: love for yourself as well as for others.

- Your WORK must be in alignment with mind and spiritual advancement, for your own well-being and in service of others as well as your Divine Creator.

- Your AWARENESS must be aligned with your physical, spiritual and mind expansion. Your must hold respect for your natural environment, the animal and plant life and Creation in general.

- Your PHYSICAL BODY must be regarded as a sacred creation and an extension of your Divine Creator. It must be respected and taken care of accordingly. A basic knowledge of its vital functions and needs is useful in selecting your individual and necessary tools for the nourishment and upkeep of your physical apparatus.

- Your TIME must be conscientiously divided between work, play, rest (sleep and meditation) and communion with your Divine Creator.

- Your ACTIVITIES must be chosen carefully and be a reflection of the positive and loving vibration of your Divine Creator.

- Your SOCIAL circle must be chosen carefully and be a reflection of the positive and loving vibration of your Divine Creator.

- You must EMBRACE all humans as your brothers and equals, while allowing each to express their individual choices and practices freely.

- Your must CONSCIOUSLY COMMUNE daily with your Divine Creator. There are no specific requirements regarding the amount of time or the method by which you dedicate your focus to the Divine. It is necessary however to be in full respect and express gratefulness and recognize the Divine Creator as your Creator-Father and the Creator of all beings and things.

THE INVISIBLE CREATES AND RULES THE VISIBLE...

Energy is invisible but it can manifest as visible. The visible becomes an extension or the material aspect of invisible energy. Therefore the invisible energy is the creator force which manifests physically and not the other way around. The energy creating the visible is therefore the "larger" aspect of the visible. Or in simple terms, what you see was created by the energy which you cannot see.

In your physical reality, you create (through thought) an energy which you cannot see. You can only see its manifestation when your thought becomes materialized. However, you can be certain that your thought initiated the creation and not vice versa. Your physical brain is unable to create another physical object on its own without thought and intent projection.

It is therefore a universal understanding that invisible energy creates visible reality. Since the creative process of materialization is innate in all intelligent beings, then you may conclude that your physical selves were created by an invisible intelligent Consciousness, which is larger or more evolved than your material self. Once created, you are linked to your energetic "parent" and will therefore share its blueprint. Through this link, your invisible Creator rules and controls your genetic makeup, your reality and destiny.

WHAT IS SELF-REALIZATION?

Self-realization is:

- The purpose and goal for entering physical reality. It is through the experience of creativity and mind expansion in the physical that you attain self-realization.

- The intimate knowledge, experience and control of your physical body and mind.

- The actual physical, mind-al and spiritual experience of the Creator-Source through the person of your Divine Creator.

- The ultimate experience of finding your self and identity as an independent consciousness simultaneously connected to your Divine Creator and His entire Creation.

- The ultimate blending experience as you physically, mentally and spiritually merge with your Divine Creator's Consciousness, which is the only bridge to the Creator-Source.

Humans are able to attain self-realization by living a true religious life and by recognizing and acknowledging their intimate link to the Divine Creator. However, you carry out your physical agreements at a different pace individually and will typically take several expressions or "life-times" to achieve self-realization. It is natural, even necessary, to co-exist with a variety of souls at different evolutionary levels so that those more evolved may assist those who require ushering and guidance.

Once you attain true self-realization, your human life will be complete and it is no longer required to incarnate physically. Your merged awareness with your Divine Creator's Consciousness will indeed lead you to higher realms of Creation and advanced spiritual expression.

10

Future Man and Future Earth

I asked all the questions I could think of regarding the "future", and my beloved teachers would repeatedly and unfailingly point to a book, a specific page and a specific paragraph that would answer my question. They are unstoppable!

Along the way, I wondered if I was some sort of prophet who would predict world events and help humanity prepare for its salvation or tribulations. As I began writing this chapter, I became the prophet I thought I was—and that everyone is—as soon as I recognized my humbleness concerning the perfection of the Divine Order.

It became clear that world events, while created by each thought each individual is having at any moment in time, are nonetheless orchestrated by the Divine Intelligence working in complacence with the Divine Order of all Creation. No one can predict tomorrow's outcome of human thought but the Divine Order can indubitably dictate the direction humanity must evolve towards if it is to maintain its equilibrium and citizenship within the whole. It is human choice and free will functioning within a divine and glorious orchestra of Life which infallibly leads us to the Love, Truth and Beauty of the one Creator-Source we call "God".

◆   ◆   ◆

Earth is supervised by a divine hierarchy of Beings who lead all destinies to their original agreement with the cosmic structure, the One Creator-Source. These divine organizations monitor all material worlds and minister the mind expansion and evolution of the species.

The divine bodies assigned to your world sit at the apex of your planetary grid, where ALL human physical, mind-al and spiritual matrixes converge. They function by controlling the energy influx and filter out, so to speak, those patterns which do not match the original Divine blueprint of the planet. They maintain and facilitate divine, interplanetary and intergalactic communications and broadcasts to insure your planet remains one with the Whole. Through these broadcasts, your governing angels are able to perfectly maintain your planet's physical, mind-al and spiritual balance and properly shape and protect your destiny. Nuclear propulsion within the Earth's grid for example, not only tears the electromagnetic fabric of your planet but it also reverberates into your neighboring solar systems and eventually your entire galactic structure. This, in turn, dangerously disrupts the gravitation, communication and distribution of life supporting structures of the entire affected system.

If interfered with or corrupted, these celestial communications will also reduce your spiritual evolution and disrupt the harmonic patterns perfectly established by your Creators. Your world then becomes quarantined and isolated.

Such is the history of your planet, where the reigning celestial bodies and their misguided followers experimented with your then-immature species and isolated it from the Whole. Therefore a system of mind control, fear, separateness, illusion of power, material gain, spiritual bondage, and such concepts as of heaven and hell, ensued. The chaos now observed on your planet is the result of such patterns established almost 200,000 years ago by these "fallen" governing agents.

Similarly, there are those bodies of Light, originating at the Creator-Source, who are responsible for restoring and maintaining cosmic harmonics and balances. These beings, such as your Divine Creator, personalize and incarnate in whatever form necessary to re-establish the unification of the worlds. These beings embody the energy of the Creator-Source itself while they incarnate in human and other material forms. Their electric charge is tremendous as to lift an extraordinary amount of energy and transmute it to its original divine blueprint. While these unique Beings appear mostly as teachers and compassionate healers, they are simultaneously executing a pattern of energetic work beyond human comprehension. They appear as one single individual when in fact, they de-particularize their energy potential in a thousand bodies in different locales and dimensions to execute their divine mission. Their real work is complete on the isolated planet when the assisted species' energetic lines are re-established with the neighboring worlds and the Creator-Source. The concept of becoming "one with God" is this very idea of eradicating corrupt influences and re-aligning your planet with the Divine Breath of the Creator-Source.

By the mere fact of entering the current human matrix, your Divine Creator allows and establishes new laws and genetic encodings. He summons the appropriate cosmic forces responsible for this tremendous shift of energies, and it is through His direct and concealed communion with the Creator-Source that He is able to encode the entire planet with the new enlightened patterns.

While He is embodied and personalized in ONE physical being, your Divine Creator's energy is fragmented into thousands of material manifestations within your Earth system and beyond its galactic boundaries. From your linear perspective, you are unable to perceive His presence or the massive energetic manipulation involved in His divine work. But you will soon come to realize that this evolved Consciousness and Person had been present and working with you. His mission is now, in fact, finished. His Divine planetary "beams" and grids have already anchored on Earth and your new divine encodings have already been activated. There is no existing force in the Universe that is capable of undoing or interfering with your imminent emergence as a new enlightened species. You will soon be observing the magnificent physical transformations this Divine Creator has instilled as He eternally secured your planet and your individual destinies within the structure of the Whole. This is what you may call the advent of a Messiah.

Your Divine Creator is assisted in this Earthly mission by spiritual as well as galactic physical beings who volunteer for such work to serve their Creator. The entire body of beings involved in this sacred endeavor form a "Dominion", not in the physical sense but in spiritual terms. Some beings are dispersed within the Earth's atmosphere or neighboring planets while others incarnate in human flesh. Their functions include planetary observation, pulse and vibratory testing and monitoring, neutralization of detrimental frequencies and the restoration of the imminent collapse of your societal structures.

The group of incarnate beings mostly assists humans with spiritual healing and guidance. However, the energetic field they are capable of channeling is so powerful that they can heal almost upon contact. Some are in full memory of their soul contract while others become cognizant of their mission when it is time to participate in the physical manifestation of this extraordinary task.

While the process of the Divine Creator's work is spontaneous, there is a time-delay, so to speak, as His work is already complete when its physical manifestation occurs before your eyes. This is due to the massiveness of light energy He carries from the Source: appearing as ONE individual Being requires the fragmentation of His energetic memory cells and when his work is complete, these fragments are re-united as to form one enormous and indestructible energy field, which can then manifest physically. This "de-particularization" process is the reason you are unable to observe His work simultaneously as it is being carried out.

In conjunction with your Creator's work is the instilment of the Creator Energy or your "Divine Mother", who is closely related and tied to His mission. The Creator Energy, while being Her own separate entity is nonetheless part of the massive matrix of your Divine Creator and comes as a direct link from the Creator-Source into the human realm. She is typically an energetic field originating from the Universal Spirit which does not materialize in one particular physical being. However, the current human evolutionary patterns required such an unusual and unprecedented phenomenon to occur upon your planet at this very time.

Extraordinarily, the Creator Energy is in fact amongst you as a physical being as well as an energetic field. Similarly to your Divine Creator, the Creator Energy de-particularizes and fragments energetically into a myriad physical beings and planetary entities within your human matrix and beyond your Milky Way and galactic structure. Upon entry in your physical system, She automatically establishes new cosmic patterns aligned with the Universal Spirit of the Creator-Source.

While Her physical manifestation and experience resemble those of your Divine Creator, Her effects are sporadic and most generalized. They are mostly concerned with the establishment of *Divine Truth* within the physical realms, thus orchestrating a series of concrete events which inevitably allow such realignment. From a practical perspective, you will observe the frequent emergence of Truths, events and circumstances which had been concealed from the mass consciousness for millennia at a time. Ignoring or defying Her powerful existence and impact will categorically lead to public scandals and forced proper human enactment.

The Creator Energy is also evenly distributed to all humans. It is the individual free-will which leads humans to negative or positive choices and actions. However, with the brilliant emergence of this powerful and divine entity within your realm, your daily interactions with others will become more truthful as you will become inclined to speak the truth and project purer thoughts. Your intensified and expanded telepathic awareness will also allow you to be in tuned with others' intent. Before long, deception on your planet will become utterly obsolete.

More importantly, the Creator Energy instilled in the hearts of all humans alike is the spiritual link between each creature and your Divine Creator. It is the gravitational pull which helps you remember and recognize Divine Truth. Finally, it is the energy which purifies your heart and leads you into this Divine Truth which must eternally prevail.

YOUR TRANSITION TIME (THE NEXT 10-YEAR CYCLE).

Your current structures will be challenged and compromised. While you are observing a negatively focused, self-seeking and materialistic world, you can hardly conceive of the physical, intellectual and spiritual attainments which characterize the highly evolved order you are moving into.

All Divine work is gradual and natural: your Earth atmosphere is changing so that it may naturally release the old programming and give birth to a new and more evolved species. As the celestial guardians hold their rhythmic frequencies, your Sun will move into a new position along with a transformational energetic field. Your Sun and Moon cycles will change and begin a new spiral movement.

Energy can never be destroyed. It can be re-created. It is of this point of re-creation that you speak. The Light source will shift too into the next rate of calibration. Your scientists have evidence of the emergence of new star systems and their original and different interactions. There are no telescopes to measure these developments which can only be perceived in your third dimensional reality after they are complete at the Source. However, you are currently and most definitively transitioning into your new subliminal state of being and while you may think that you must exist in a realm of duality, you can be assured that your survival and emergence as an evolved and free species has been secured.

The re-positioning of Earth's orbit and planetary alignment is essential for the implanting of the new encodings brought forth by the human presence of your Divine Creator and the Creator Energy. These colossal shifts have triggered the Earth energetic grids to "split". The layers which frequencies resonate with the Universal Truth will remain and re-unite with the Whole, while the energies in disharmony will disintegrate and permanently self-obliterate.

In practical terms, all current energies are accelerated to their rapid consequences. War, for example, which is fabricated in the fearful and guilty minds, is imminent now because of the energetic momentum it has already accumulated. However, its history will carry itself out and rapidly self-obliterate as it is unequivocally balanced by the emergence of the new energies. These new energies will quickly neutralize, so to speak, the desolating effects of your looming devastations.

The encoding of your new species, which is the very encoding of the Divine Creator himself, can be simplified as follows:

a. All humans become one with the Creator-Source.

b. All humans have equal rights in soul expansion.

c. All humans are allowed expressions per their evolutionary and vibratory pattern; in other words, free will.

d. The only programs governing this planet are the Universal and Cosmic laws of the Creator-Source.

e. All humans are liberated from the program of bondage currently in existence.

f. The governing divine bodies are of the Creator-Source and are working to instill the new human species with Divine Love, Truth and Beauty.

g. All existence is an extension of the Creator-Source which created it. All rebellion and opposing forces will naturally isolate themselves and rapidly self-obliterate.

The current human race is not capable of expanding to such acceptance and understanding at this time. It must evolve into another type of species, characterized by a "bigger" brain which allows such information to be stored and retrieved. This brain and consciousness expansion of humans and the entire Milky Way galaxy have been activated by the re-alignment of energetic lines with the rest of the Cosmos. As the Divine Creator and his assisting forces hold their rhythmic patterns, new star systems are emerging and this world and the human species will begin interacting in a new a different way.

Those individuals resisting this evolutionary and necessary change will succumb to the most difficult trial of existence: the choice of accepting their Creator-self and merging with the Oneness of the Cosmos or fading away in the self-annihilation and shadows of their own fears.

As you are awakening to your new reality, you will gradually observe that all current institutions which are still based on the old programming will become obsolete by the time your transition is complete. Your selfish and corrupt government, banking and corporate officials, while appearing to be functioning cohesively, will quarrel and disband and make room for the evolved sentient beings who are here in the true service of humankind. Soon enough, all organized institutions, religious and educational structures that no longer serve your true spiritual evolution will disintegrate and make room for a new and enlightened system.

Before long, you will begin to recognize that all humans on this planet, without any exception, already belong to a planetary and Universal Citizenship and Truth. Your monetary system will be re-directed and allocated to the exploration and proper distribution of natural resources for the cleansing and nourishment of the planet and its children. Your military will slowly disintegrate but will eventually converge to create one Earthly force within a controlled and peaceful galactic confederation. You will voluntarily live by your oath to love others as you love yourself, and care for the Earth as you care for your own home.

YOUR FUTURE POTENTIAL (2013 TO 2035).

Your current structures will disintegrate entirely. It is the time for the adjucation of the New Age. Once your transition is complete, you will be living in an evolved society, based on a fair and intelligent natural resources system, in full compliance, respect and harmony with the Earth Mother as well as the Cosmic Order of the Divine Source. You will indeed be experiencing life from an entirely new perspective.

The knowledge that all reality is in fact an energetic vibrational "orchestra" becomes ordinary, while inter-galactic communication and broadcasts with other planets and future worlds will become commonplace.

You will understand and use the Universal Laws to create the physical reality you desire. You will be able to master your thoughts and creative powers, manipulate energetic fields to control your physical bodies, and experience spontaneous healing. This will be a disease-free society where death becomes a natural transition, accomplished by deliberate and conscious preparation.

Your future physical body and appearance will hardly change. However, your physical brain will expand your capability to retrieve and process complex information and knowledge. Your memory bank will be enhanced by the understanding that all are one with the Creator-Source and you will able to recall your soul contracts while in the flesh so you can consciously carry out your divine agreement.

Your sleep and rest requirements will be reduced and your vision and hearing will expand as to allow the convergence of the senses and the experience of a multi-sensory and multi-dimensional physical life. You will become experienced in commanding and controlling your outer reality, and will easily discern the existence of all types of intelligent beings and energy fields: material, transitory and spiritual.

Your spirit of unity will overshadow your need to acquire unnecessary material goods. While your artistic aspirations will continue expanding, your perception and abuse of the material will certainly be overcome. Natural energy will be available to all and therefore material transactions can be carried out only through voluntary trade.

You will also grow more generous and altruistic. You will share your homes with families of different ancestry. Your education will revolve around human psychology, spirituality, the study of the arts, sciences and the cosmos. Your laws of human enactment and punishment will become utterly obsolete as you become masters of your emotions and senses. You will expand your spirituality to a degree that is unimaginable to you now. Your technological and scientific advancements will become aligned with service for humankind, soul emancipation and Spirit Self-realization.

FINALLY...

Regardless of your history, you are magnificent intelligent beings who have chosen this incarnation to enhance your planetary functioning and expand your spiritual awareness en masse. This is your sacred agreement and a powerful co-creation began when the Divine Forces combined with your Collective Consciousness in your planet's energetic shift. It is Man's "asking" and your Divine Creator "giving" for the purpose of Oneness with the rest of the Cosmos and the Creator-Source of all Beings and Things. It is, indeed, the ultimate experience of Joy and Love.

PART II

INTENT, PRAYERS AND DREAMS:
Practical Tools

Introduction to Prayers

PRAYER is a focused intent or thought which you put forth for the purpose of materializing your desire. It is the process of summoning Source Energy which accelerates and brings about your desire.

Before you begin to call on the Cosmic Forces, you must acquire an understanding of how energy is manipulated through your prayer. In addition to fully grasping the concepts discussed in Part I of this book, you must also become aware of the laws and principles which accelerate the materialization of your prayer or "asking".

As you pray, your focused thought generates a vibration, an electromagnetic charge, which also reflects your intent. The Universal Beings and Forces responsible for converting theses vibrations into new forms of energy, material or otherwise, respond to your focused thought and intent by matching your vibrations perfectly with their different potentials. This includes bringing into your physical experience information, individuals or thoughts which constitute the answer to your prayer. For example, you may be asking for a new job and the assisting cosmic agencies may manifest an ad in the newspaper, a phone call from a friend or your boss may suddenly decide to promote you. While you do not observe the work of the invisible agencies, they are nonetheless responsible for these physical manifestations which you may label as luck or coincidences.

Your prayer is therefore prompting invisible beings and forces to manipulate invisible energy into manifestation. The speed of these manifestations depends upon the electromagnetic charge of your intent and focus. With time and practice, you will realize that you are capable of praying and manifesting within a relatively short time if not spontaneously.

How to Summon the Cosmic Forces of the Universe

The following guidelines will help you be as clear and specific as possible while you allow the forces of the Universe to provide you with the most appropriate and perfect response to your prayer.

1. You must hold in your awareness and during your prayer, the inner knowing that *you are an extension of your Divine Creator*. You are energetically linked to his Being and therefore to ALL of His creative powers and forces. There is an energetic link between you and Him and by focusing your words into a prayer you are deliberately activating this energetic frequency which is sacred and powerful.

2. Your asking must be held in your consciousness for a minimum of ~~14~~ seconds which will automatically launch and activate the forces in the Universe responsible for converting the energies necessary for materialization. You are a *co-creator:* You must ask and the Universal Forces must provide, for it is Law.

   65sec

3. You must know which energies you are inviting in your prayer experience and those which you are not. Many invisible beings may be attracted to you while you pray and choose to interfere or distract your work. Therefore, you must *consciously invite* your Spirit Self and those beings aligned with your intent and the energy of the Creator-Source and reject those that are not. You must consciously create your prayer space without unnecessary distractions.

4. Your asking must have *clear intent, focus and precision.* Specific *asking and intending* are powered with an electro-magnetic charge which accelerates their manifestation as opposed to unfocused or generalized ones. For example, "I ask for peace on Earth" is barely significant compared with "I

ask and intend the safety of my family members, Joe, Patricia and Mike who are caught in _____ (name of war zone)".

5. Be specific about *the nature and purpose* of your asking but you need not determine the means by which it must manifest. For example, you may be clear about a particular promotion at your workplace. However, you may not be aware of other circumstances more suited for your career advancement. You may say: "I ask and intend to manifest this _____ promotion or be presented with similar opportunities to support my career advancement" rather than "I want this particular promotion".

6. Your asking must be aligned with the *betterment of your spiritual and mind-al self.* For example: "I ask and intend to manifest this high paying job in order to stimulate my intellect and mind, improve my communication and creative skills or management experience with others..."

7. Your asking must be aligned with *the betterment and welfare of others.* This intent is the same as the above, but the prayer is now aligned for others.

8. Your asking must *add to the quality of your life* and that of others.

9. Your asking must *be respectful of all of your Creator's Creations* which means your asking may not interfere or be detrimental to others choice and mode of expression.

10. Finally, you must be *grateful for the grace* you are receiving as prayer is your personal communion with the Divine and the acknowledgment of your inner link to your Divine Creator. The energy behind true and honest gratefulness is an extremely powerful precursor for manifestation. It is charged with a highly positive and loving vibration which the Universal Forces match powerfully and instantaneously.

With the above checklist you can insure that your prayers are powerfully directed with precision and force. An additional important element to consider is *writing down* the prayer as you are projecting it mentally. The action of writing not only enhances your focus but also carries your intent out into the physical medium. Ideally, you may want to write down your desires and repeat them a few times until you feel you are complete. If aligned particularly with your spiritual betterment and that of humanity, you can be certain that your words and actions will be immensely and quite promptly answered. Prayers of more selfish or destructive nature are not only detrimental to the collective consciousness but also to your own self-realization and spiritual growth. In this case, while your egotistical prayers may manifest, your residence in the lower physical realms may also be prolonged rather than accelerated.

Creating Your Past/Creating Your Future

Your past experiences are a set of frequencies which you carry with you in one form or another. These frequencies can be in the shape of a thought or a physical imbalance which will trigger emotional upset until they are addressed and cleared. While you are unable to eliminate the individuals or circumstances of your past, you *are* able to transmute the frequencies attached to them and be relieved from their burden.

Any frequency which still stands in the way of creating your future can be addressed and transmuted. That is the process of altering or creating your past and can be achieved by following these guidelines. If performed accurately, you should be able to manipulate your past as you desire in one setting or at least in a relatively short time.

- Identify a current problem or challenge which you want to overcome.

- Ask for and intend to reach the resolution of your problem.

- Identify the emotion attached to the problem or challenge.

- Retrace your past experiences which are similar or will remind you of this very emotion attached to your problem or challenge.

- Continue going back in time to the very first experience this particular emotion has surfaced in your life. It may be during adolescence, as early as 3 years old; or possibly, at birth.

- Carefully examine the circumstances, individuals and feelings attached to this first experience.

- Allow yourself to go through these emotions by being fearful, angry etc.

- Now, ask to perceive this same experience from the perspective of the individual who or the circumstances which harmed you or triggered this negative emotion. If you are able to do this exercise properly, you will most likely realize that their intention was coming from their own lack or weakness.

- Make a choice about what you want to do with this experience.

- Begin to feel compassion towards the individual by noticing their weakness or ignorance which prompted their behavior.

- Once you truly feel compassion, you have successfully transmuted the negative emotion attached to the experience into one which is aligned with your current intent.

Throughout this exercise, you may summon the assistance of your Spirit Self and the spirit guardians to enhance your clarity. It is also helpful to work with another individual who will reflect your story from an objective perspective and therefore allow more precision and clarity throughout the process.

While you cannot eliminate the people and circumstances in your past, you can eliminate the frequency attached to such experiences. The patterns which you carried through until this day will simply vanish. That is the meaning and process by which you, as a powerful creator, are able to alter your past and begin to create your future.

Dreams: Use and Applications

The world of dreams is a necessary medium for your consciousness to explore your non-physical reality, cleanse and filter your fears and negative thoughts, as well as remember your pre-natal agreement. It is a purposeful guidance system and can be utilized consciously as follows:

1. Before you retire, ask one question which is most important to you and request to "see" the answer through your dreams. Due to the energetic momentum your daytime thoughts create, you will most likely not receive your answer at once. It may require you a few days or up to several months depending on how "cluttered" your consciousness is with other distracting thoughts. However, as you become proficient at the exploration of your consciousness, you will be able to ask the question and immediately receive your answer in your dream. In fact, your human mind is created as to operate in such a manner. Because the world of dreams is highly misinterpreted and misunderstood, it is also rarely put to its proper use to benefit your spiritual growth.

2. As you awaken, make an effort to recall your dream and begin translating it in your physical conscious language. Remember, your dreams are subjective and symbolic. For example, if you dream of a snake, find out what a snake means or represents to you rather than revert to its literal meaning. More importantly, it is crucial to remember the *emotions* and feelings attached to each element of your dream as these emotions carry the answer and the meaning of your experience.

3. When dreaming of disturbing or upsetting events, you may consider analyzing the fears attached to such experiences and consciously request to revert or transmute them. If you realize that dreaming of your own death for instance is particularly disturbing, you may ask to transmute that fear into a comforting and non-threatening experience. You may also ask that the

concept of your death not interfere with your physical and emotional wellbeing. You are able to create the reality you desire. Therefore, consciously transmuting such fears into positive thoughts is not only possible but in order as it is dictated by the Laws of Creation.

4. Some individuals do not recall their dreams and believe they simply do not have them. However, all human consciousness operates in similarity and navigates through the invisible worlds with the same patterns. You may ask to remember your dreams so that you begin to take full advantage of the guidance and messages your Spirit Self is conveying to you.

SAMPLE INDIVIDUAL PRAYERS

1. Prayer for Self-Realization & Spiritual Expansion

I am here now in communion with my Divine Creator and the Cosmic Forces of the Universe for the purpose of manifesting my desires as follows:

* I ask and intend my Spirit Self and those beings of the highest Love Energy to be present and offer me guidance now.

* I ask and intend that those beings who are distracting or in conflict with my intent be banned from my experience now.

* I ask and intend assistance from my Spirit Self, my Spirit Masters and Guides in manifesting and clarifying my spiritual path. I ask to remain focused on what I am here to do in order to expand my spirit, mind and consciousness.

* I ask and intend that my daily thoughts and actions be directed and aligned with my Spirit Self and the pure energy of my Divine Creator.

* I ask and intend to be the conduit of the Love energy and vibration so it may serve me on my spiritual path, be of service to others and in turn my Divine Creator.

* Finally, I am grateful for the grace I receive each day as I acknowledge my Divine Creator's presence in my inner being and in all other beings and things equally.

And so it is.

2. Prayer for Love and Harmony

I am here now in communion with my Divine Creator and the Cosmic Forces of the Universe for the purpose of manifesting my desires as follows:

* I ask and intend my Spirit Self and those beings of the highest Love energy to be present and offer me guidance now.

* I ask and intend that those beings who are distracting or in conflict with my intent be banned from my experience now.

* I ask and intend to experience the Love vibration through all that I do, say and think and through my interactions with others.

* I ask and intend that the Love vibration be dominant in my life now so it may reflect the presence of the Divine Creator.

* I ask and intend that Love and Harmony be primary in my daily environment and that those that I come in contact with may also benefit from the presence of the Divine Creator.

* I am grateful for the Love and Harmony present in my life now and ask to be the conduit of the Love and Harmony of my Divine Creator for myself as well as for others.

And so it is.

3. Prayer for Protection & Guidance

I am here now in communion with my Divine Creator and the Cosmic Forces of the Universe for the purpose of manifesting my desires as follows:

* I ask and intend my Spirit Self and those beings of the highest Love energy to be present and offer me guidance now.

* I ask and intend that those beings who are distracting or in conflict with my intent be banned from my experience now.

* I ask and intend that I reflect the Love energy of the Creator and be continuously surrounded by His Light and vibration so I may remain protected by Him.

* I ask and intend that I only attract energies and individuals aligned with the Creator's Wisdom and Love who will protect me from distracting or harmful influences.

* I ask and intend that I remain focused on my Divine Creator's Energy so I may naturally and intuitively be protected and guided by His Light.

* I acknowledge my Divine Creator as my protector and guide and am grateful for His Love and Wisdom. I ask than I continue reflecting His energy so I may offer protection and guidance for others as well.

And so it is.

4. Prayer for Clarity

I am here now in communion with my Divine Creator and the Cosmic Forces of the Universe for the purpose of manifesting my desires as follows:

* I ask and intend my Spirit Self and those beings of the highest Love energy to be present and offer me guidance now.

* I ask and intend that those beings who are distracting or in conflict with my intent be banned from my experience now.

* I ask and intend that my Spirit Self provide me with clarity so I may identify the areas in my life which need improvement.

* I ask and intend that my Spirit Self offers me clarity in _____ area, so I may make the proper decisions aligned with my higher good and that of others.

* I ask and intend clarity regarding the choices in the _____ area of my life so I may identify the different options that I may have.

* I ask and intend clarity of purpose for the _____ area in my life so I may see and feel that it is perfectly aligned with my highest good and that of others.

* I am grateful to be an instrument of clarity for others so I may also help them make the appropriate decisions on their spiritual journey and allow them to be an instrument of clarity for me.

And so it is.

5. Prayer for Inner Peace

I am here now in communion with my Divine Creator and the Cosmic Forces of the Universe for the purpose of manifesting my desires as follows:

* I ask and intend my Spirit Self and those beings of the highest Love energy to be present and offer me guidance now.

* I ask and intend that those beings who are distracting or in conflict with my intent be banned from my experience now.

* I ask and intend that my inner being feel peaceful and harmonious with my environment and Universe.

* I ask and intend that fear, anxiety of any similar feelings disappear from my experience or be transmuted to positive and uplifting feelings.

* I ask and intend that I attract peaceful thoughts and experiences so that my inner self may feel in perfect harmony with the Universe.

* I am grateful for the opportunity to offer peaceful thoughts and wishes to others so the peace of my inner self may be reflected in theirs.

And so it is.

6. Prayer for Physical Wellbeing and Good Health

I am here now in communion with my Divine Creator and the Cosmic Forces of the Universe for the purpose of manifesting my desires as follows:

* I ask and intend my Spirit Self and those beings of the highest Love energy to be present and offer me guidance now.

* I ask and intend that those beings who are distracting or in conflict with my intent be banned from my experience now.

* I acknowledge that I have innate healing powers and that my physical body is able to correct itself naturally. I ask and intend that my physical wellbeing and good health be restored now.

* I ask and intend that my physical body be aligned and reflect the Love of my Creator so I may feel and experience his presence in every aspect of my physical body.

* I ask and intend that my _____ (problem area) be restored to its normal and natural physical health now.

(Repeat the above for every area in your physical body which needs attention).

* I ask and intend that my physical body feel good, vibrant and healthy now.

* I ask and intend emotional and mental strength to support my physical body and keep me confident in restoring my body's normal and natural well-being and balance.

* I acknowledge and am grateful for the grace I have received in restoring my physical well-being and good health.

And so it is.

7. Prayer for Mental Balance and Emotional Comfort

I am here now in communion with my Divine Creator and the Cosmic Forces of the Universe for the purpose of manifesting my desires as follows:

* I ask and intend my Spirit Self and those beings of the highest Love energy to be present and offer me guidance now.

* I ask and intend that those beings who are distracting or in conflict with my intent be banned from my experience now.

* I ask and intend to release all fears and negative thoughts that may interfere with my mental and emotional well-being and balance.

* I ask and intent that my mental and emotional balance and well-being be restored now.

* I ask and intend to attract positive and uplifting energies so I may reflect my own joy onto others.

* I ask and intend to be relieved from distracting and obsessive thoughts which hinder my mental and emotional well-being.

* I am grateful for the positive aspects and gifts I have and ask to attract more joyful and uplifting experiences into my life and that of others.

And so it is.

8. Prayer for Financial Security

I am here now in communion with my Divine Creator and the Cosmic Forces of the Universe for the purpose of manifesting my desires as follows:

* I ask and intend my Spirit Self and those beings of the highest Love energy to be present and offer me guidance now.

* I ask and intend that those beings who are distracting or in conflict with my intent be banned from my experience now.

* I ask and intend to attract all potential and appropriate circumstances and individuals who will provide me with financial and material opportunities and freedom.

* I ask and intend to be guided and attract the most appropriate and beneficial circumstances which will allow me to create and expand my financial freedom.

* I ask and intend to feel positive and joyful about my financial potential so that I may attract more financial opportunities into my physical experience.

* I am grateful for my past and current financial accomplishments and wish to increase my finances to my maximum potential.

* I acknowledge that my intent for financial freedom is in alignment with my spiritual growth and that of others.

And so it is.

9. Prayer for Material Success and Security

I am here now in communion with my Divine Creator and the Cosmic Forces of the Universe for the purpose of manifesting my desires as follows:

* I ask and intend my Spirit Self and those beings of the highest Love energy to be present and offer me guidance now.

* I ask and intend that those beings who are distracting or in conflict with my intent be banned from my experience now.

* I ask and intend to attract all potential and appropriate circumstances which will provide me with better shelter (home) and _____ (car, clothing…) opportunities.

* I ask and intend to make the appropriate decisions which will lead me to material security and success.

* I ask and intend that my fears and distracting thoughts not interfere with my potential to attract and secure material freedom and success.

* I am grateful for my past and current material accomplishments and ask to expand my material success and potential.

And so it is.

10. Prayer for Career Development

I am here now in communion with my Divine Creator and the Cosmic Forces of the Universe for the purpose of manifesting my desires as follows:

* I ask and intend my Spirit Self and those beings of the highest Love energy to be present and offer me guidance now.

* I ask and intend that those beings who are distracting or in conflict with my intent be banned from my experience now.

* I ask and intend to attract all appropriate work opportunities which will benefit and support my career growth.

* I ask and intend to attract individuals and circumstances that will allow me to expand my creative, artistic or management skills (list others).

* I ask and intend that my career development be in line with my spiritual growth so I may enrich my life and that of others.

* I am grateful for the work and career opportunities I have created so far and ask for more choices which will enhance my intellectual and professional skills.

And so it is.

11. Prayer for Romantic Relationships

I am here now in communion with my Divine Creator and the Cosmic Forces of the Universe for the purpose of manifesting my desires as follows:

* I ask and intend my Spirit Self and those beings of the highest Love energy to be present and offer me guidance now.

* I ask and intend that those beings who are distracting or in conflict with my intent be banned from my experience now.

* I ask and intend to attract a romantic relationship which is based on unconditional love and spiritual maturity.

* I ask and intend to give and receive love and share a harmonious and loving relationship with another being that will reflect and complement my attributes, skills and accomplishments.

* I ask and intend that this relationship be effortless and in perfect alignment with both our spiritual paths and our mind/soul expansion.

* I ask and intend that this relationship be an uplifting daily co-creation and a joyful and positive experience for both.

* I am grateful for all the love I am now experiencing in my life and ask to share my life intimately with my soul counterpart.

* I ask and intend that this romantic union be a daily reminder and reflect the loving spirit of our Divine Creator.

And so it is.

12. Prayer for Work-Related Relationships

I am here now in communion with my Divine Creator and the Cosmic Forces of the Universe for the purpose of manifesting my desires as follows:

* I ask and intend my Spirit Self and those beings of the highest Love energy to be present and offer me guidance now.

* I ask and intend that those beings who are distracting or in conflict with my intent be banned from my experience now.

* I ask and intend to attract a nurturing and healthy work environment so that I may thrive and improve my skills at my workplace.

* I ask and intend that my exchange with my co-workers be courteous, professional, caring, friendly etc...(name the attributes you wish to create).

* I ask and intend that those individuals (you may mention specific individuals) who appear negative or distracting allow me to grow and learn from their experience in a joyful manner.

* I ask and intend to be professional, friendly, supportive (name the attributes you wish to create for yourself) towards my co-workers so that I attract the same experience in return.

* I am grateful for the positive and supportive individuals who have helped me at my workplace thus far and ask to continue attracting similar healthy and uplifting circumstances which will allow me to thrive and grow at my workplace.

And so it is.

13. Prayer for Healthy Family Relationships

I am here now in communion with my Divine Creator and the Cosmic Forces of the Universe for the purpose of manifesting my desires as follows:

* I ask and intend my Spirit Self and those beings of the highest Love energy to be present and offer me guidance now.

* I ask and intend that those beings who are distracting or in conflict with my intent be banned from my experience now.

* I ask and intend that I get along with my _____ (family members) as best as possible and to resolve our differences in love and harmony.

* I ask and intend to be responsible for my own emotions and experiences and refrain from blame or victimization from past experiences.

* I ask and intend to release all negative emotions pertaining to _____ (incident) or _____ (family member) so I may be free mentally and emotionally.

* I ask and intend to forgive myself for _____ (experience) as well as _____ (family member associated with incidents) and acknowledge my own as well as their spirit wholeness and perfection. I accept _____ actions as being misguided and inappropriate and ask for their emotional recovery and release.

* I am grateful for those family relationships which provided me love and support and wish to let go of those experiences which no longer serve my spirit expansion and soul purpose.

And so it is.

14. Prayer for Creative Work

I am here now in communion with my Divine Creator and the Cosmic Forces of the Universe for the purpose of manifesting my desires as follows:

* I ask and intend my Spirit Self and those beings of the highest Love energy to be present and offer me guidance now.

* I ask and intend that those beings who are distracting or in conflict with my intent be banned from my experience now.

* I ask and intend to attract the highest creative and uplifting circumstances to support and help me in my work _____ (painting, writing…)

* I ask and intend that I remain in a positive, clear and focused state to generate the most and highest quality creative ideas and thoughts.

* I ask and intend to attract all appropriate sources of inspiration which will enhance my creative work _____.

* I ask and intend that all negative and distracting thoughts not interfere with my creative process.

* I am grateful for the inspiration and sources of creativity and growth and ask to be the conduit of Divine creativity in my work _____.

And so it is.

15. Prayer for Pro-Creation and Child Bearing

(This prayer is mostly effective and beneficial when recited with your partner)

I am (We are) here now in communion with my Divine Creator and the Cosmic Forces of the Universe for the purpose of manifesting my desires as follows:

* I ask and intend my Spirit Self and those beings of the highest Love energy to be present and offer me guidance now.

* I ask and intend that those beings who are distracting or in conflict with my intent be banned from my experience now.

* I ask and intend that this child be the outcome of our mutual love and intent for spiritual growth.

* I acknowledge that procreation is a sacred act of love between my partner and me, as well as with our Divine Creator. I ask and intend to regard this new child as a continuation and extension of Life from our Divine Creator and as a gift from Him.

* I ask and intend that all physical and emotional experiences associated with childbearing and child birth be pleasant and comfortable as they are in alignment with the love of our Creator.

* I ask and intend to attract an emotionally, mentally and physically healthy and balanced being that will enrich our lives and contribute to our spiritual growth.

* I ask and intend to give unconditional love and respect to this new child as he/she is a reminder of the sacred act of Creation of our Divine Creator.

* I am grateful for the blessings and love in my life and ask to extend my joy into the life of my child and those around me.

And so it is.

16. Prayer for Ill Individuals and Children

(This prayer is mostly effective and beneficial when recited with your partner or with an intimate group)

I am (we are) here now in communion with my Divine Creator and the Cosmic Forces of the Universe for the purpose of manifesting my desires as follows:

* I ask and intend my Spirit Self and those beings of the highest Love energy to be present and offer me guidance now.

* I ask and intend that those beings who are distracting or in conflict with my intent be banned from my experience now.

* I ask and intend for _____ (name of ill person or child) to find relief from his/her symptoms of _____ (illness).

* I ask and intend to be the conduit of Divine Love and Light and positive emotions and to project this divine energy onto _____ (name).

* I ask and intend for _____ (name) to receive Divine guidance and love to help her/him restore her/his _____ physical, mental, emotional health well-being and balance.

* I ask and intend that all negative, distracting or fearful influences be banned from _____ (name) experience now.

* I ask and intend for that the Cosmic Forces of the Universe restore _____ (name) physical, mental and emotional balance now.

And so it is.

SAMPLE COLLECTIVE PRAYERS

1. Prayer for Peace and Spiritual Emancipation

We the people are here now gathered in prayer to summon the spirit of our Divine Creator and the Cosmic Forces of the Universe to support us in manifesting Peace and Spiritual Emancipation in our society now.

* We ask and intend that the forces of Love and Light be present with us to protect and guide us in our prayer now.

* We ask and intend that the forces of Darkness be neutralized by the powerful Light of our Divine Creator and His governing forces in our world now.

* We ask and intend to resolve our issues and differences in a peaceful manner and to realize our spiritual unity and connectedness.

* We ask and intend to attract positive circumstances for the resolution of _____ (conflict) and receive the necessary help and support for the resolution of _____ (conflict).

* We are grateful for the blessings our nation/group has received and ask for more loving guidance and peace from our Divine Creator.

And so it is.

2. Prayer for the Prevention and Relief from Violent Acts, Terrorism and Wars

We the people are here now gathered in prayer to summon the spirit of our Divine Creator and the Cosmic Forces of the Universe to support us in manifesting peace and harmony among the people of this Earth.

* We ask and intend that all humanity be *protected* from acts of violence, wars and terrorism at all times.

* We ask and intend that we remain focused on *peaceful and positive thoughts* so we may only attract peaceful and positive circumstances and experiences.

* We ask and intend to *alleviate the suffering* of those who experience acts of violence, wars and terrorism and those families and friends who witness such acts, to be helped and guided by the Light of our Divine Creator through their physical and spiritual journey.

* We ask and intend *forgiveness* for those responsible for these deliberate acts of violence, wars and terrorism and ask to allow them to find the Light and Truth of our Divine Creator.

* We the people summon the Love and Light Forces of the Universe to protect us in this prayer as it is being carried out and keep away the shadows and darkness and those who carry that intent.

* Finally, we acknowledge that all experiences are in perfect Cosmic Order and in perfect alignment with the Creator-Source. We are therefore thankful to be the conduit of Love and Light and to be of service to humanity as we also serve our Divine Creator.

And so it is.

3. Prayer for Presidential Elections, Political Fairness & Stability

We the people are here now gathered in prayer to summon the spirit of our Divine Creator and the Cosmic Forces of the Universe to support us in manifesting our next _____ (country) presidential elections of _____ (year) as follows:

* We ask and intend that the new candidate (or current administration) be *truthful* and *respectful* of the lives of the people.

* We ask and intend that the new candidate (or current administration) be respectful of our Earth's needs and environment and begin taking serious steps in saving the *environment* from all toxic human-induced substances.

* We ask and intend that the new candidate (or current administration) begin exploring *natural resources* as a means to provide shelter and feed our Earth population in lieu of dependence on oil and other toxic and costly substances.

* We ask and intend that the new candidate (or current administration) resolve international crisis in a *peaceful* manner, NOT through war and unnecessary armament. We ask that our administration embraces people from all cultures and all religions as ONE human population intending to live in peace and harmony on this Earth.

* We ask and intend that the new candidate (or current administration) be *financially responsible* and appropriately redirect spending to support imminent issues, social security, education...NOT selfish and corrupt corporate agendas.

* We ask and intend that the *truth be told* regarding intentional clandestine experimentations and research including laser, weapons, mind control techniques, identity control, extraterrestrials etc., which may be harmful in any way to ANY human, animal or mineral life on our planet.

* We ask and intend that no action be taken or support in favor of any law (national or international) or any world government or banking system which will infringe on individual *personal identity* and personal life.

* Finally, we the people summon the Love and Light Forces of the Universe to protect us in this prayer as it is being carried out and keep away the shadows and darkness and those who carry that intent.

* Through this prayer, we the people are thankful to be a conduit of Love and Light as we usher humanity into the new age. We are thankful to be of service to humanity as we serve our Divine Creator.

And so it is.

4. Prayer for Economic Growth and Cultural Expansion

We the people are here now gathered in prayer to summon the spirit of our Divine Creator and the Cosmic Forces of the Universe to support us in manifesting economic growth and cultural expansion.

* We ask and intend that the forces of Love and Light be present with us to guide us and protect us in our prayer now.

* We ask and intend that the forces of Darkness be neutralized by the powerful Light of our Divine Creator and His governing forces in our world now.

* We ask and intend to attract the appropriate opportunities and potential to support our economic growth and cultural expansion.

* We ask and intend to give and share our knowledge with other less fortunate groups so they may benefit from our experience and expertise and reflect back their economic and cultural success onto us.

* We ask and intend to remain aligned with the divine codes of fairness so that our success may also bring about the success of others.

* We are grateful for our group's economic and cultural strength and successes and ask to further expand our experience of emancipation and growth.

And so it is.

5. Prayer for Technological and Scientific Advancement

We the people are here now gathered in prayer to summon the spirit of our Divine Creator and the Cosmic Forces of the Universe to support us in manifesting economic growth and cultural expansion.

* We ask and intend that the forces of Love and Light be present with us to guide us and protect us in our prayer now.

* We ask and intend that the forces of Darkness be neutralized by the powerful Light of our Divine Creator and His governing forces in our world now.

* We ask and intend to attract all opportunities and appropriate knowledge to support and enhance our technological and scientific advancement.

* We ask and intend to remain aligned with the Divine light in our quest and use of technological advancement. We ask and intend that technology and science be used for the highest good of the people and with integrity and love.

* We ask and intend that new knowledge be shared with all the people of this Earth so that all may benefit equally.

* We are grateful for the technological and scientific knowledge we have received and ask to further our education and quest for such knowledge.

And so it is.

6. Prayer for Animal, Plant and Mineral Life

We the people are here now gathered in prayer to summon the spirit of our Divine Creator and the Cosmic Forces of the Universe to support us in manifesting economic growth and cultural expansion.

* We ask and intend that the forces of Love and Light be present with us to guide us and protect us in our prayer now.

* We ask and intend that the forces of Darkness be neutralized by the powerful Light of our Divine Creator and His governing forces in our world now.

* We ask and intend respect for animal, plant and mineral life and protection from unnecessary human experimentation, abuse and destruction.

* We ask and intend that animal, plant and mineral life be allowed the freedom and quality of life they deserve and contribute to the growth and beauty of our planet.

* We ask and intend that animal, plant and mineral life exist in harmony with humans on this planet and contribute to the growth and spiritual expansion of the species.

* We are grateful for the beauty and perfection of our animal, plant and mineral life and ask for guidance in our daily interaction and co-existence with them.

And so it is.

FINAL NOTES FROM THE TEACHERS-AUTHORS

The information enclosed herein is a revelation of Truth from the perspective of Divine Beings originating at the Creator-Source. It is delivered with the assistance of the writer who is our vibrational match in your physical system. It is intended to expand your awareness beyond your current understanding of life on Earth and establish your spiritual oneness and link with your divine ancestry. While your interpretation of this text will be subjective, the message is nonetheless irrefutable and absolute.

Your current scientific approach to resolving an infinite reality is limited to the physical aspects of life's mechanisms and mysteries. If science, by definition, is the study of the physical Universe and the physical aspects of life, then your sciences are appropriate indeed. However, material reality and principles are perpetually created by the Universal-Mind. Unless your sciences bridge the gap between material proof and divinity by integrating the realm of Creator-Probability and Multi-Dimensionality into their reasoning, your sciences will remain a discipline of only one aspect of human life, its physical facet alone.

Divine Intelligence and Consciousness work with precision and purpose and it is intended for this text to be revealed at this required time and this required space. As you begin to observe the new truths behind your current religious, social, economical and political establishments, this material will become more relevant and useful to your self-realization. The expansion of the mind to this plane of understanding will enable you to put into a new perspective every daily chore that seems insurmountable at times. This new perspective is a bird's eye view of your own journey and the explicit way of releasing your fears and uncertainty. On the other hand, this book is delivered at a time when humanity is becoming exposed to a new form of communication. As dictated by the Divine Truth for evolutionary beings, your telepathic and psychic awareness is due to expand drastically. Thus the knowledge and understanding of the invisible worlds as they operate within your system will usher you into safe and comforting grounds of your new reality.

ABOUT THIS BOOK

Message excerpts received from my Spirit Friends and Teachers regarding the writing this book...

"The best way to describe how the material is being revealed is through levels of awareness called trances in human terms. You may wish to include information on the fact that you hear all revelations but the true work is done by focusing into an energetic field which connects you to a frequency familiar to you called the Divine Father."

"The beneficial part of your book is that it is written in a language that the common man must and will comprehend. The scientific and technical details you refer to are not necessary at this stage."

"Child of Heaven, you are acquiring first hand knowledge which is valuable to the highest degree to the human population now on Earth. Your physical location is of utmost importance for the manifestation of this material as it determines which frequencies can interpolate with your energetic vibration..."

"You are not letting me relay the importance of this material and continuously ask to compare your work with that of others. Your work is of another call. It is coded with a Divine blueprint. I am asking that you trust that the order and the pace ARE the freedom which you must have to receive other information. Your book is purposely revealed in segments as you are accessing many "dimensions" simultaneously and the work is harder than it appears. The pace of the writing and editing works perfectly with our harmonics."

"Let this be your proof and physical manifestation of who you truly are which is indeed the son and spirit daughter of the Divine Father. His energy is being revealed through you and this book which will also reveal your divine secrets. Life on Earth is finished in one capacity and beginning in a huge way on another level of intelligent interactions and loving relationships. All is perfect indeed."

"This book's impact on the spiritual movement currently on Earth will bring a newer version of reality which has not been explored prior to this time. It is the revelation and philosophy of the next order. It is of prime importance to manifest now. It is of GOD. It is of Life itself, the Creator-Source of all that exists."

"Through this book, you are the conduit of the Love Energy of the Divine Father...the inequities which you realize in your mind about what you should know and what you already have will be graciously resolved and the mysteries of your beingness of God will be complete. The ambiguity comes from your lack of proof and manifestation but you are nonetheless of the Love vibration, the Divine order that which is pure and eternal."

"This book will be in its entirety when it is appropriate to sell it. If we continue feeding it with new information that cannot be used at the present time, it will defeat its purpose as part of the process is to integrate others' understanding so the information can be received and understood appropriately. You now have a reasonable amount of information that is ready to be handled and if you increase this amount at this point in time, it will only be cluttering and confusing to others who will read it."

"Your book is about the revelation of new and powerful energetic fields which you are creating with your powers and all that you are will bring the harmonic balance to this plane of existence. All that you read is nothing more than acknowledgment of what you already know. The way you present this material will encompass all that you know until now and will lead humanity to its further development. You do not recall the details of this role at this time and that is because you are now focused physically. But when you surrender your focus onto your Spirit Self, trust that you will be revealed all that you need to proceed with your writing."

"You are here to occupy a tremendous power. The book is about you in a sense that it is mirrored by your human experience and revealed that way in human terms but the part of you revealing the information, needless to say, is attached to the Energy of the Creator-Source of ALL humans."

GLOSSARY

ASKING: Prayer, intent.

COSMIC MIND: Mind Energy of the 7 spirit aspects of the Creator-Source.

CREATOR ENERGY: Energy of a Divine Being that possesses higher creative powers.

CREATOR-SOURCE: God, All That Is, Universal Creator of all existence.

DIVINE FATHER: Creator Being of the universes and realities Earth is part of. He is the expression/body of the Creator-Source.

DIVINE MOTHER: Creator Being of the universes and realities Earth is part of. She is the spirit aspect of the Creator-Source.

EVOLUTIONARY BEINGS: Material and physical beings whose consciousness must evolve in order to blend with the Creator Consciousness.

MIND ENERGY: Energy of the collective psyche.

SPIRIT ENERGY: Energy of the collective spirits.

0-595-33343-5

Printed in the United Kingdom
by Lightning Source UK Ltd.
120089UK00002B/256

9 780595 333431